French

George W. Barnie
Principal Teacher of Modern Languages, Inverness High School

Jérôme Lestienne
Teacher of French, Inverness High School

With thanks to Harriette Lanzer,
author of GCSE Bitesize Revision: French, first published in 1998

Published by BBC Educational Publishing, BBC White City,
201 Wood Lane, London W12 7TS
First published 1999, Reprinted 2000, Reprinted 2001, Reprinted 2002
© George Barnie and Jérôme Lestienne/BBC Worldwide (Educational Publishing) 1999

ISBN: 0 563 46492 5

Designed by Malena Wilson-Max.
Illustrations by Tribal Design
Printed in Great Britain by Bell & Bain Ltd., Glasgow

Questions you might be asked

In your speaking assessment you will be asked lots of different questions. Here are some possible questions. You'll find some sample answers at the beginning of the answer section (page 80).

1 *Qu'est-ce que tu fais pendant le week-end?*
   What do you do at the weekend?

2 *A quelle heure est-ce que tu te lèves pendant les vacances?*
   What time do you get up in the holidays?

3 *Qu'est-ce que tu fais le jour de ton anniversaire?*
   What do you do on your birthday?

4 *Tu aimes ton collège? Pourquoi (pas)?*
   Do you like your school? Why (not)?

5 *Qu'est-ce qu'il y a à voir et à faire dans ta ville/ton village?*
   What is there to see and do in your town/your village?

6 *Qu'est-ce qu'il y a pour les jeunes dans ta ville/ton village?*
   What is there for young people in your town/your village?

7 *Quelles sont les différences entre la cuisine française et la cuisine écossaise?*
   What are the differences between French food and Scottish food?

8 *Combien d'argent de poche est-ce que tu reçois?*
   How much pocket money do you get?

9 *Qu'est-ce que tu fais après le college?*
   What do you do after school?

10 *Tes parents, qu'est-ce qu'ils font dans la vie?*
   What do your parents do for a living?

11 *Qu'est-ce que tu fais comme travail?*
   What job do you do?

12 *Qu'est-ce que tu préfères, partir en vacances en famille ou avec des copains/copines? Pourquoi?*
   What do you prefer, going on holiday with the family or with friends? Why?

13 *Qu'est-ce que tu vas faire à l'avenir?*   What are you going to do in the future?

14 *Tu manges au self au collège? Pourquoi (pas)?*
   Do you eat in the school canteen? Why (not)?

15 *Comment tu fais pour aller au collège?*
   How do you get to school?

Contents

BITESIZEfrench

Teenage concerns   56

Extra listening   72

Extra grammar   76

Revise.

Introduction

About BITESIZE

Standard Grade French BITESIZE is a revision guide to help you with your Standard Grade exams. You can watch the TV programmes, work on the activities and even dial up the internet on-line service.

If you don't have the TV programmes, simply miss out the listening sections and concentrate on the other skills – but you may still want to have a look at the tips that are given. You might get access to the internet through your school. If not, don't worry, there's still a lot for you in this book.

It's called BITESIZE because that's a good way to revise – in small chunks. The book is divided into small sections so that you can go through them one-by-one. You can plan out your own revision programme or simply brush up on the sections you don't know very well.

BITESIZE is not a course book. It is to be used in addition to all your notes and other work you have done in school.

❗ REMEMBER This book aims to help you improve your grade in the exam. It gives you the basics you need to know for Standard Grade, but you'll also need to revise from your classwork, so check with your teacher that you're revising everything you should!

About this book

The book is divided into three large sections, covering all the topics required for Standard Grade French. The topics covered are exactly the same as the ones on the video – and they are in the same order, making it easier for you to find. Each large section is subdivided into BITESIZE sections:

A Daily life	**B Holidays and travel**	**C Teenage concerns**
1 Home and family	1 Directions	1 The world of work
2 Jobs around the house	2 Travel	2 The environment
3 Pocket money	3 Hotels and campsites	3 Healthy living
4 Daily routine	4 Eating out	4 People and personal relationships
5 School	5 Shopping	
6 Plans to go out	6 Clothes	
7 Leisure	7 Weather	

■ In each section you'll find listening activities based on the video.

■ There are reading sections – some are very short and others are much longer. Each reading activity is marked with the symbol **f/g** or **g/c** (i.e. Foundation/General or General/Credit). Choose the one which is right for your level.

■ As you know, writing is optional. If you're not sure whether you're doing writing or not, check with your teacher. If you're not doing the writing exam, just skip the writing sections!

■ Speaking at Standard Grade is worth 50% of your final grade. By March you'll have done several speaking assessments and your teacher will have a final grade for you. If you don't have to do any more speaking activities, simply miss that section out.

KEY TO SYMBOLS

📺 A link to the video

❓ Something to think about

◎ An activity to do

f/g A Foundation/General activity

g/c A General/Credit activity

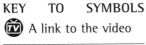

Vocabulary and grammar

In each section there's a vocabulary list. These lists don't include words which are too similar to the English (such as *football, badminton* etc.) and you'll still need to revise vocabulary given in class. This book will remind you of some very basic words and expressions and will also introduce you to some new up-to-date ones (e.g. how to say 'surfing the net'). The vocabulary sections as well as the grammar ones are BITESIZE – so that you don't ever suffer from indigestion!

Be ready

<u>Throughout your planned revision</u>, make sure that:

- you work in a quiet environment
- all you need is within reach (jotters, books, pencils, the video and a dictionary)
- nothing can distract you (computer games, the TV, your little brother ...)
- you have a break frequently – only have one bite at a time.

<u>On the day</u> ('days' is more accurate), make sure that:

- you have a good breakfast (how about some croissants to get yourself into a 'French' mood?)
- you know where to go, and when
- you have a few pens and pencils, a dictionary (if not provided)
- you do the questions you know first – don't waste time on a question you find too hard, go back to it later
- you time yourself and don't panic – do your best and at least try everything.

Bonne révision et bonne chance!

REMEMBER Getting ready for an exam is like getting ready for a performance – the end result is you showing what you can do and making the most of what you know.

THE ON-LINE SERVICE You can find extra support, tips and answers to your exam queries on the BITESIZE internet site. The address is http://www.bbc.co.uk/ education/revision

This section is about

• Tips to help you revise

This section will give you an idea of what is expected of you in each part of your Standard Grade exam. It will also give you ways in which you can start preparing right now.

Here are a few tips on how to approach the different sections – Reading, Writing, Speaking and Listening. Throughout the book there are BITESIZE tips in the margins to remind you of some of the most important points.

Reading

■ Always read the introduction to the passage.

■ Read the questions before you start reading the passage – then you'll know what information you're looking for.

■ When you're in the exam, divide your time equally for each passage.

■ Leave plenty of space so that you can go back and change your answer or add to it.

■ Before you look up any words in the dictionary, go through the passage (or part of a long passage) spotting words and phrases you know. Then look for words and phrases that are like English.

■ Underline in pencil words you think you might have to look up to help you answer the questions.

■ Remember to use the French section of the dictionary to look the words up.

■ It will be difficult to find verbs – don't panic! There are plenty of other words that you will find.

■ Each reading activity is marked **f/g** (Foundation/General) or **g/c** (General/Credit) in BITESIZE. Decide which is the best for your level.

■ In your exam, many of the reading passages are taken from newspapers and magazines. The ones in this book are fictitious, but they're in the same style.

■ You are allowed to use a dictionary in the reading exams. It's best to have your own so that you know how it's organised. Check with your school which they recommend.

■ Look carefully at what you've been asked to do. Do not leave blanks – make an intelligent guess.

■ Make sure your answers make sense!

Writing

■ If you're not sitting the writing exam, you can skip the writing sections.

■ Write what you have practised many times in class.

■ Only use the dictionary for the odd word: you can't write an essay from a dictionary.

■ Try to think of what you know in French. Don't think in English and then translate.

■ Remember what you've learnt for speaking – you can use that for writing too.

■ Learn how to transform a simple sentence into

a more complex one – you'll find out how in BITESIZE.

- There's a list of topics that come up again and again at General level – make sure you know what they are.

- Have a store of useful words and phrases at your fingertips which you could place almost anywhere.

- Keep your writing quite simple unless you're absolutely sure of what you're doing.

- Most of the time, you'll be writing in the present tense. Why not revise the present tense? See the Grammar section or dial up the internet.

Speaking

- Speaking at Standard Grade is worth 50% of your final grade, so it's worth spending time practising this skill.

- Your on-going assessment normally starts right at the beginning of S4. If your speaking assessments are all over, skip these sections and revise some other aspects of your French.

- These sections of BITESIZE only give you an idea of what is expected of you. Why not look at the video? Or try the internet.

- In the book there are tapescripts of the same kind of speaking assessment done by different pupils – one Credit, one General and one Foundation. Try recording some of them.

- To improve your performance:
  - try to use as many sentences as possible
  - give as much information as you can
  - ask questions (there is a section on how to ask questions in the book)
  - prepare well (get out all your notes and prepare in advance)
  - if you don't understand, learn a few sentences to ask for repetition of a question (e.g. **Comment? Répétez s'il vous plaît.**)
  - think ahead (what could they ask you?).

- Always look at the teacher when you speak. Be as involved as possible.

- Normally you speak in the present tense. Check your knowledge of the present tense in the **Grammar section**. There is a fuller presentation on the internet.

Listening

- The best way to prepare for this exam is to:
  - get as much practice as possible (use the video of the Bitesize French programmes, if you have it.)
  - learn your vocabulary (you will not have a dictionary in this exam).

- Concentrate on what you do know. You know a lot. There will be lots of words and phrases you do understand.

- Revise or learn all the vocabulary in this book as well as your classwork. It will help you a lot.

- Read the questions before the cassette starts so that you know what you are listening for.

- In the exam you will hear the French twice. When you practise, listen as often as you like.

- Before watching the video, look at the vocabulary section of the same unit first.

- Remember – at all levels you are listening for the main point or points, not every single word.

- Try and think ahead. Look at the question – what might the answer be? Then listen to what the French actually says. Make sure your answer makes sense.

- For those who have no access to the video, there are a few tapescripts in this book. You or someone else could read the tapescript onto cassette, then you could work from that.

Daily life

This section is about

- Home and family
- Pocket money
- School
- Leisure

- Jobs around the house
- Daily routine
- Plans to go out

Reading a postcard from a friend

◎ *f/g*   Your French penfriend has written a postcard introducing himself.

! REMEMBER
Don't worry about handwriting – there are no handwritten versions in the exam.

Salut!

Je suis ton nouveau correspondant français. Je suis né à Paris, mais maintenant, j'habite à Calais, dans le nord de la France. J'ai quinze ans, et mon anniversaire est le douze août. Physiquement, je suis assez petit avec les cheveux bruns et les yeux verts. Ma sœur, qui est plus âgée que moi, est professeur de français dans mon collège! Écris-moi vite.

Philippe.

Sarah Johnson
17 Lenox Road
Leeds L12 7MQ
UNITED KINGDOM

Hi!
I'm your new French penfriend. I was born in Paris, but now I live in Calais in the north of France. I'm 14 and my birthday's on the 11th of August. I'm very small with brown hair and grey eyes. My brother, who is older than me, is a French teacher at another school.
Write soon.
Philippe

Sarah Johnson

17 Lenox Road

Leeds L12 7MQ

UNITED KINGDOM

On the left is the English translation of the postcard, but there are six mistakes in it. Try to spot them and underline them.

(Total: 6)

VocabularyZONE

◎ These phrases will be really useful for your exam, so see if you can try and learn them!

Home and family

La famille   The family

ma tante   my aunt

ma mémé   my granny

mon pépé   my grandad

mon arrière-grand-père
  my great-grandfather

ma belle-mère   my step mother

mon demi-frère   my step brother

Je suis enfant unique.   I'm an only child.

Je n'ai pas de sœur.   I don't have any sisters.

A la maison   At home

la salle de séjour   living room

la salle à manger   dining room

la cave   cellar

l'entrée   hall

mon bureau   my desk

la chambre d'ami   spare room

les lits superposés   bunk beds

au rez-de-chaussée   on the ground floor

au premier étage   on the first floor

il y a   there is/are

Décrire la ville   Describing town

Elgin, c'est ...   Elgin is ...

beau (belle)   beautiful

tranquille   quiet

joli(e)   nice

assez petit(e)   quite small

vivant(e)   lively

sale   dirty

Jobs around the house

Je fais le ménage.   I do the housework.

Je fais mon lit.   I make my bed.

Je range ma chambre.   I tidy up my room.

Je fais la vaisselle.   I do the dishes.

Je passe l'aspirateur.   I do the hoovering.

Je sors les poubelles.   I take the bins out.

Je charge/vide le lave-vaisselle.
  I load/unload the dishwasher.

Je mets le lave-linge/sèche-linge en route.
  I put on the washing machine
  /tumble dryer.

Je fais le repassage.   I do the ironing.

Je fais les courses.   I do the shopping.

Pocket money

Je reçois cinq livres par semaine.
  I get £5 a week.

Je ne reçois pas d'argent de poche.
  I don't get any pocket money.

Je fais des économies.   I save my money.

Je ne travaille pas.   I don't work.

Je dépense mon argent en CD.
  I spend money on CDs.

Je travaille dans un magasin.
  I work in a shop.

Je gagne mon propre argent en faisant du baby-sitting.   I make money babysitting.

J'ai un petit boulot.   I've got a part time job.

Je distribue des journaux.   I deliver papers.

◎ Learn one list of words at a time, then work with a friend to test each other.

There is more useful vocabulary on page 15.

Moving house

◎ ⓣⓔ Your penfriend's parents are thinking about moving. You have a look at the four advertisements the estate agent has given them. Answer the questions below to make sure you understand them.

A

A vendre, 3km Marseille. maison 60m². orientation sud. jardin 200m². vue sur mer. chauffage central gaz. meublée partiellement avec garage. deux chambres, cuisine, salon. vente cause décès. 400.000F.
tél. 04.39.54.11.10.

B

A louer, Paris 16ème. appartement style moderne. 3ème étage. quatre grandes chambres. deux salles de bain. salon. grande cuisine équipée. vue sur Tour Eiffel. chauffage électrique. 9.000F par mois.
tél. 01.31.68.00.18.

C

A vendre dans bocage normand. ancienne ferme restaurée sur terrain 1570m². deux étages. séjour, cuisine amenagée, trois chambres, salle de bain, deux WC, garage. grenier aménageable. chauffage fuel. Prix à débattre.
tél. 03.60.75.86.33.

D

A louer, près de Disneyland. petit village (St Myrien). magasins à proximité. appartement deux pièces, rez-de-chaussée. tout confort. 3.000F par mois.
tél. 01.43.63.10.27.

! REMEMBER
Read the questions first. Check the marks allocated to each question. If there are two marks, write two pieces of information. Be careful if you write more than two – you will be penalised if one is wrong.

1 Which one(s) are for sale? (2)

2 What kind of heating system has advertisement B? (1)

3 Why are they selling/renting house A? (1)

4 Why is there no price for C? (1)

5 Why are *Disneyland* and *magasins* mentioned in D? (1)

6 Your penfriend's parents are interested in the former farm on two floors with an attic. Which advertisement is it? (1)

(Total: 7)

Weekly chores

◎ *t/g*   Your penfriend shows you the list of weekly duties he has to do if he wants pocket money. Match the list on the left with the pictures on the right.

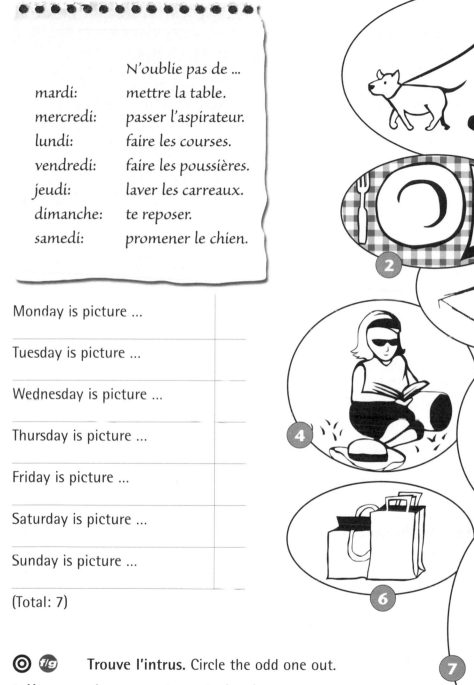

N'oublie pas de ...

mardi:	mettre la table.
mercredi:	passer l'aspirateur.
lundi:	faire les courses.
vendredi:	faire les poussières.
jeudi:	laver les carreaux.
dimanche:	te reposer.
samedi:	promener le chien.

Monday is picture ...

Tuesday is picture ...

Wednesday is picture ...

Thursday is picture ...

Friday is picture ...

Saturday is picture ...

Sunday is picture ...

(Total: 7)

◎ *t/g*   **Trouve l'intrus.** Circle the odd one out.

1 **House:** maison, appartement, chambre, caravane.

2 **Family:** oncle, tante, cousin, frère.

3 **School:** cours, histoire-géographie, professeur, EPS.

4 **Leisure:** ordinateur, console, magnétoscope, manette de jeu.

Pocket money

◎ **g/c**   Your penfriend sends you this letter telling you about his pocket money.

> J'ai de la chance : mes parents me donnent de l'argent de poche chaque semaine. Bien sûr, cinquante francs, ce n'est pas beaucoup, mais ça suffit pour aller au ciné ou voir un match de foot au stade municipal. Parfois, je demande un peu plus d'argent à ma mère pour m'acheter des CD ou des jeux pour ma console vidéo. Mais ma mère dit que je dois faire des économies. Alors je crois que je vais prendre un petit boulot le week-end à la piscine. C'est mal payé, mais c'est toujours mieux que rien!

1 How often does he get pocket money?   **(1)**

2 How much does he get?   **(1)**

3 What does he do with it?   **(2)**

4 What does he want to buy with the extra money he asks for?   **(2)**

5 He is planning to get a job at the swimming pool at the weekends. What does he say about it?   **(1)**

(Total: 7)

◎ **f/g**   Find the French for the following expressions in the wordsearch: video recorder, week, music, savings, swimming pool, month, to sell, to rent, furnished, to buy.

! **REMEMBER**
Go through the passage spotting words you know and words you can guess from English.

```
M A G N E T O S C O P E
U A J K C W K E B M I X
S L A F O X Q M K E S C
I O C H N Y H A E U C L
Q U H M O I S I J B I U
U E E G M G I N A L N Y
E R T H I Z T E V E E O
W Z E V E N D R E V D D
U I R C S K O P A Z Q I
```

BITESIZEfrench

Daily routine

Je me réveille à ...   I wake up at ...

Je me lève.   I get up.

Je me lave.   I wash.

Je prends une douche.   I have a shower.

Je m'habille.   I get dressed.

Je me maquille.   I put my make up on.

Je prends le petit déjeuner.   I have breakfast.

Je quitte la maison.   I leave the house.

Le collège commence à ...   School starts at ...

Saying when/how often you do things

tous les jours   every day

quelquefois/parfois   sometimes

d'habitude   usually

souvent   often

toujours   always

avant/après le dîner   before/after dinner

pendant la journée   during the day

entre 19 heures et 20 heures
   between 7pm and 8pm

School

les matières   school subjects

l'EPS (éducation physique et sportive)   PE

la géo   geography

l'EMT (éducation manuelle et technique)
   technological studies

les sciences nat   biology/geology

le bâtiment   the building

le concierge   janitor

le proviseur   rector

l'adjoint   depute head

le/la prof de français   French teacher

la salle d'anglais   English room

le self/la cantine   self-service/canteen

les devoirs   homework

Plans to go out

Ici Jenny!   It's Jenny!

C'est bien Marcel?   Is that you Marcel?

On sort demain?
   How about going out tomorrow?

Tu veux sortir samedi?
   Do you want to go out on Saturday?

Je regrette.   I'm sorry.

Si tu veux.   It's up to you.

Rendez-vous où?   Where will we meet?

Devant le cinéma.   In front of the cinema.

A quelle heure?   At what time?

D'accord.   All right.

A samedi alors.   See you on Saturday.

Qu'est-ce que tu fais dimanche?
   What are you doing on Sunday?

Qu'est-ce que tu veux faire?
   What do you want to do?

Leisure

faire de la planche à voile   to windsurf

je surfe le net   I surf the net

manette de jeux   joystick

un jeu vidéo   video game

un lecteur CD   a CD player

un ordinateur   computer

faire des photos   to take pictures

écouter des CD   to listen to CDs

regarder un film au magnéto(scope)
   to watch a movie on video

filmer au caméscope
   to film with a camcorder

envoyer/recevoir un fax
   to send/receive a fax

Daily routine 1

◎ *f/g*　Your penfriend Philippe has written you a letter about his daily routine. Unfortunately, your dog got it first and ripped it up. Try to put the pieces (sentences 1–12) together so that they match the pictures.

1　Je vais à la cantine à midi.

2　Je prends le petit déjeuner à sept heures trente.

3　Je fais mes devoirs de dix-sept à dix-huit heures.

4　Je m'habille à huit heures.

5　L'école commence à huit heures trente.

6　Je regarde un film à vingt heures trente.

7　Je prends le bus pour l'école à huit heures et quart.

8　Je me lave à huit heures moins le quart.

9　Je prends le dîner à vingt heures.

10　Je me couche à vingt-deux heures quinze.

11　Je me réveille à sept heures et quart.

12　Je mange le goûter à seize heures trente.

(Total: 12)

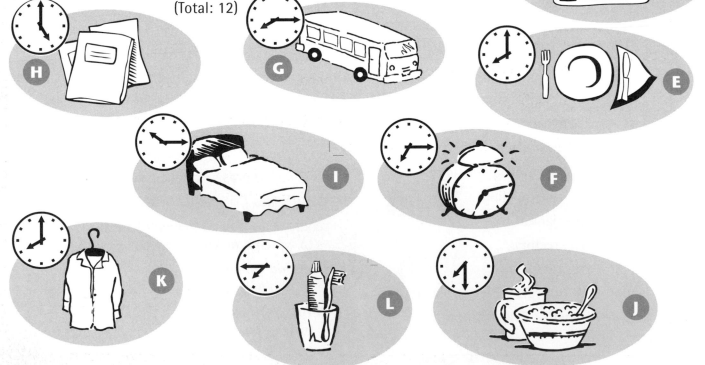

Nouns and articles

Genders: *le/un* = masculine, e.g.   *le/un crayon*   the/a pencil

                  la/une = feminine, e.g.   *la/une douche*   the/a shower

In French, some words are masculine, some are feminine. There's often no real reason. You just have to learn the gender with each noun. In a dictionary this is usually marked next to the noun as *(m)* for masculine and *(f)* for feminine.

Plural: *les crayons*   the pencils

             les douches   the showers

             des copains   some friends

- Try to learn the gender *(le/la)* with the noun.
- *Les* (the) and *des* (some) are used in the plural for both masculine and feminine nouns.
- There are some rules for plurals. In many cases, an *-s* is added to the noun, but there are exceptions such as:

        le jeu ⇨ *les jeux*

        Un animal ⇨ *des animaux*

When speaking about people's jobs, you don't need *le, la, un* or *une*, e.g.

        Mon frère est mécanicien.   My brother's a mechanic.

        Ma sœur est médecin.   My sister's a doctor.

The words for 'my' in French are:

        mon + masculine noun

        ma + feminine noun

        mon + any noun beginning with a vowel (whether masculine or feminine)

        mes + plural noun (more than one)

Daily routine 2

◎ g/c   When he hears what happened to the letter he wrote (page 16), your penfriend decides to re-write it. However, he adds more details to it. Read the letter and answer the questions.

(page 16)

> Salut! Ça va ?
>
> Je t'écris pour te raconter une de mes journées typiques. Chaque matin, je me réveille vers sept heures et quart, ensuite je prends des céréales au petit déjeuner. En général, je suis toujours un peu en retard et je rate le bus de huit heures et quart. Alors je dois courir pour arriver au collège à huit heures et demie.
>
> J'ai de la chance – dans certains collèges, le premier cours est à huit heures ! A midi, je mange généralement à la cantine du collège, mais ce n'est pas bon, alors parfois avec des copains, on se paye un MacDo.
>
> Les cours finissent à quatre heures. Ma mère me prépare un bon goûter composé de tartines à la confiture et un bol de chocolat chaud. Après ça, je dois faire mes devoirs, ce qui me prend environ une heure : j'ai horreur de ça. En France, on mange le dîner plus tard qu'en Ecosse : entre dix-neuf et vingt heures. A vingt heures, toute la famille regarde le journal, c'est l'équivalent du journal de dix-huit heures en Ecosse. Enfin, le film du soir commence vers vingt heures trente, et je me couche tout de suite après. Cependant, le week-end, j'ai le droit de regarder la télé ou sortir plus tard, car je peux faire la grasse matinée le lendemain.
>
> Au revoir!

REMEMBER For a longer letter like this, take it in small sections. Underline in pencil words you think you might have to look up to help you answer the questions. (Remember to use the **French** section of the dictionary!)

REMEMBER Check the marks for each question – for two marks, write two pieces of information.

1 What time does he get up in the morning?   (1)

2 What does he have for breakfast?   (1)

3 What does he have to do when he is late in the morning?   (1)

4 Why does he say he is lucky to start school at 8.30am?   (1)

5 Where does he sometimes go for lunch? Why?   (2)

6 What does his mum prepare for him after school?   (2)

7 What does he hate?   (1)

8 What does he say about dinner in France?   (1)

9 What is on TV at 8pm?   (1)

10 What is he allowed to do at the weekend?   (2)

(Total: 13)

Timetable

You have a look at your penfriend's timetable. His **emploi du temps** is slightly different from yours. First, try to spot the differences.

	lundi	**mardi**	**mercredi**	**jeudi**	**vendredi**	**samedi**
08h–09h	français	perm.	EPS	hist/géo	anglais	éd. civique
09h–10h	allemand	dessin	musique	anglais	maths	biologie
10h–11h	maths	anglais	technologie	français	perm.	hist/géo
11h–12h	physique	biologie	perm.	français	technologie	–
12h–13h	déjeuner à la cantine			–	déjeuner à la cantine	
13h–14h	EPS	français	physique	inform.	dessin	
14h–15h	EPS	hist/géo	perm.	allemand	perm.	
15h–16h	–	anglais	français	–	allemand	
16h–17h	–	éd. civique	–	–	maths	

perm. : permanence   hist/géo : histoire/géographie   éd. civique : éducation civique   inform. : informatique   La bibliothèque sera ouverte du lundi au jeudi de dix heures à quinze heures trente.

Now answer the questions about the timetable.

1 How many times a week does he have German? **(1)**

2 Where does he have his lunch? **(1)**

3 a What days will the library be open? **(1)**

   b What are the opening hours? **(1)**

4 Below is the same timetable, in English this time. Unfortunately, the publisher missed out some periods. Using the timetable in French, can you fill in the English one with the missing subjects? There are ten missing. **(5)**
(Total: 9)

	Monday	**Tuesday**	**Wednesday**	**Thursday**	**Friday**	**Saturday**
08h–09h	French	free	PE	hist/geo		PSE
09h–10h			music	English	maths	biology
10h–11				French	free	hist/geog
11h–12h	physics	biology	free	French		–
12h–13h	lunch			–	lunch	
13h–14h	PE	French	physics		art	
14h–15h	PE	hist/geog	free		free	
15h–16h	–	English		–	German	
16h–17h	–	PSE	–	–	maths	

French schools

◉ flg   Your penfriend writes to you about the French school system. Answer the questions.

20

❗ REMEMBER Look at the questions first. To help you identify the answer, line numbers are given on the left-hand side. There will <u>not</u> be line numbers in your exam.

1 En France, on va d'abord à l'école maternelle à partir de

2 trois ans jusqu'à l'âge de six ans. Ensuite, on va en

3 primaire. Vers onze ans, c'est le collège, où il y a un prof

4 différent pour chaque matière. Vers quinze ou seize ans,

5 on commence à aller au lycée, et en terminale, vers dix-huit

6 ans, on doit passer un examen important qui s'appelle le

7 baccalauréat ou bac. Si les résultats ne sont pas assez

8 bons pendant une année, on doit redoubler une ou

9 plusieurs fois. Après ça, on peut continuer à l'université

10 ou chercher du travail.

11 L'école en France est obligatoire jusqu'à l'âge de seize

12 ans comme en Ecosse.

1 At what age do French pupils start primary school? (lines 2–3)   (1)

2 What does he say about *le collège*? (two things, lines 3–4)   (2)

3 When do they have to take a major exam? (lines 5–7)   (1)

4 What can they do once they have passed the exam? (two possibilities) (lines 9–10)   (2)

5 What do they have to do if their results are not good enough? (lines 7–9)   (1)

6 At what age can they legally leave school? (lines 11–12)   (1)

(Total: 8)

Adjectives

Adjectives are also known as describing words. They change their ending to agree with the person, place or thing being described – if it is masculine, the adjective will be masculine; if it is feminine, the adjective will be feminine.

Regular adjectives

The most common pattern is:

–	for masculine singular	*le grand garçon* (the big boy)
+ -e	for feminine singular	*la grande fille* (the big girl)
+ -s	for masculine plural	*les grands garçons* (the big boys)
+ -es	for feminine plural	*les grandes filles* (the big girls)

Adjectives which already end in -e are the same for both masculine and feminine, e.g.
un exercice facile   an easy exercise
une question facile   an easy question

Adjectives which end in -s or -x do not change in the masculine plural form.
Il est gallois.   He is Welsh.
Ils sont gallois.   They are Welsh.

Some adjectives double their last letter when feminine.
Il est italien.   He is Italian.
Elle est italienne.   She is Italian.

Most adjectives come after the noun they are describing.
Il a les yeux verts.   He has green eyes.

But some common adjectives come before the noun.
Ma petite sœur.   My little sister.
Mon vieux pote.   My old mate.

Irregular adjectives

Many common adjectives are irregular and have to be learnt individually. Here is a list of some common ones:

masculine singular	feminine singular	masculine plural	feminine plural
blanc	*blanche*	*blancs*	*blanches*
vieux *	*vieille*	*vieux*	*vieilles*
beau *	*belle*	*beaux*	*belles*
long	*longue*	*longs*	*longues*
nouveau *	*nouvelle*	*nouveaux*	*nouvelles*

* Note that some of the above irregular adjectives have a different masculine ending when used before a noun that starts with a vowel or a silent 'h'.
un bel avion   a beautiful plane
un vieil hélicoptère   an old helicopter
un nouvel aéroport   a new airport

Birthday presents

◎ *f/g* Your penfriend writes to tell you what he got for his birthday and what he already owns.

22

❗ REMEMBER You don't need to understand every word, just enough to get the information you're asked for. Look for clues in the rest of the letter.

❗ REMEMBER If you're looking up words in a dictionary, it might be difficult to find verbs – don't panic! You can probably work them out from the rest of the sentence.

> Pour mon anniversaire, ma mère m'a acheté deux jeux vidéos pour ma console. Ils sont géniaux.
>
> L'un d'entre eux est un jeu de football. C'est pratique, parce qu'on peut y jouer à quatre en même temps. Alors, avec mes copains, on passe des heures devant l'écran à rejouer la Coupe du Monde '98. Je choisis toujours l'équipe du Brésil, car ce sont les meilleurs.
>
> L'autre jeu est un jeu d'aventure. Il faut trouver un trésor sur une île et tuer les pirates.
>
> J'ai aussi un ordinateur, en fait c'est un PC. Il est relié à l'internet, alors je peux communiquer avec des jeunes du monde entier. C'est aussi utile pour faire mes devoirs, car il y a beaucoup de documentation sur tout et n'importe quoi.
>
> Et toi? Es-tu relié à l'internet?
>
> On pourrait surfer le net ensemble et s'e-mailer.

Below is the same letter, but in English, and a few words are missing.
Fill in the blanks. A blank may be a word or a phrase.

For my birthday, I got _____ from my mum. The football game is good because_____.

When we play World Cup '98, the team I pick is_____ because_____. In the adventure game you have to _____ and _____.

My PC is connected to the internet, so I can communicate with _____. The computer is useful for _____ as there is a lot of _____. If you have the internet, we could _____ and _____.

(Total: 10)

Films

Your penfriend is describing a very famous movie of the late 1990s, but he can't remember its title. Read his letter and see if you can refresh his memory by finding the title.

> Ça se passe sur le plus gros bateau du monde, vers 1912. C'est une histoire d'amour impossible entre une riche et un pauvre qui voyagent vers les Etats-Unis. Mais il y a un accident : le bateau heurte un iceberg et il coule. C'est très romantique, mais c'est long : plus de trois heures. Le film s'appelle ... ?

Title: _____

While in France, you want to go the pictures. First, you read these film reviews to help you make up your mind.

🎬 a Le Triangle des Disparus

Film d'aventure britannique.
Durée : trois heures et quart.
« Un bateau disparaît dans le Triangle des Bermudes. Une équipe de sauveteurs tente de les sauver. »
Un suspens insoutenable !

🎬 b Le Coup de Gant

Film dramatique français.
Durée : une heure trente.
« Un ancien boxeur décide d'aider un jeune champion touché par la drogue. »
Un film triste et touchant.

🎬 c Plus près des Etoiles

Film de science-fiction américain.
Durée : deux heures dix.
« Une navette spatiale découvre une nouvelle civilisation sur Mars comparable à la nôtre. » Beaucoup d'effets spéciaux réussis.

1 Which film would you avoid if you didn't like long films? **(1)**

2 You're usually keen on movies about space conquest. Which one would you pick? **(1)**

3 You particularly like special effects. Which movie should suit you? **(1)**

4 One of the three movies has a sad story. Say which one and briefly why. **(2)**

5 What does the reviewer say at the end about *Le Triangle des Disparus*? **(1)**

(Total: 6)

●●● Writing

Writing practice

If you're not doing the writing exam, just skip this section.

In the General Writing exam you are just asked to write a few sentences. In the Credit exam you have to write an essay – approximately 200 words.

 R E M E M B E R If you're not sitting the writing exam, you can skip this section.

 Write a postcard to your penfriend, briefly introducing yourself. Use the postcard in the reading section (page 10) to give you ideas.

 R E M E M B E R A postcard is short and to the point.

 Write one sentence about each item given below. Sample sentences are given in the answer section at the back of the book.

Name

Age

Birthday

Brothers and sisters

Hobbies

Your daily routine

School

Pets

Things you don't like doing

Weekend

Holidays

This is the first letter to your penfriend. Fill in the blanks from the words given at the end of the letter. Check your answers at the back of the book.

Salut!

Je suis ta nouvelle correspondante. Je m'appelle Jane et j'ai seize _____. Mon anniversaire est le _____ mai. Physiquement, je suis assez _____ avec les cheveux _____ et les yeux marron. J'ai un _____ qui s'appelle Murray et qui est plus âgé que moi : il a _____ ans. Il est étudiant à l'université d'Aberdeen. Il étudie la _____. Mes parents sont _____. Mon père habite à Glasgow, mais ma mère et moi habitons à Peterhead. Peterhead se trouve à cinquante _____ d'Aberdeen. Mon père est au chômage et ma mère est _____. Si tu veux me téléphoner, mon _____ est le 01779 479108. Je partage une _____ avec mon frère, mais en ce moment, il loue une chambre à Aberdeen. Pendant les vacances, je vais _____ mon père. Il habite une grande _____ à Glasgow. Il s'est remarié et a deux _____ qui s'appellent Mark et Jim. J'_____ aller à Glasgow, car il y a plein de choses à voir et à faire.

(Total: 16)

adore, ans, biologie, blonds, chambre, chez, divorcés, enfants, frère, grande, ingénieur, kilomètres, maison, numéro, premier, vingt

Now try writing a similar letter with details about yourself.

_____

_____

_____

_____

_____

_____

_____

_____

_____

REMEMBER Most of the time, you'll be writing in the present tense. Why not revise the present tense now? See the Grammar section or dial up the internet. The address is on page 7.

Speaking practice

If you have finished your Speaking tasks, just miss this section out. If you are just about to go into S4, this section will give you a good idea of what is expected of you.

Talking about yourself and asking questions about people

You must be able to answer the following questions and others about yourself (the <u>underlined</u> words should be replaced with <u>your own details</u>). You should also learn the questions so that you can ask questions as well as answer them, making the dialogue more lively.

❗ REMEMBER Speaking at Standard Grade is worth 50% of your final grade.

1   *Comment t'appelles-tu?* (What's your name?)

    Je m'appelle <u>Paul.</u>

2   *Quel âge as-tu?* (What age are you?)

    J'ai <u>quinze</u> ans.

3   *Où habites-tu?* (Where do you live?)

    J'habite à <u>Dundee</u> en Ecosse.

4   *Tu as des frères et des sœurs?* (Do you have any brothers and sisters?)

    <u>Oui, j'ai un frère et deux sœurs.</u>

5   *Comment s'appelle ton frère? Ta sœur?* (What are their names?)

    <u>Mon frère</u> s'appelle <u>Philippe</u>.

❗ REMEMBER Normally you speak in the present tense. Check your knowledge of the present tense in the Grammar section. There is a fuller presentation on the internet.

6   *Tu as un animal à la maison?* (Do you have any pets?)

    <u>J'ai deux chiens.</u> / <u>Je n'en ai pas</u>. (I have two dogs. / I don't have any.)

7   *Qu'est-ce que tu aimes faire pendant le week-end?* (What do you like doing at the weekend?)

    Le week-end, j'aime <u>aller en ville et jouer au foot.</u>

8   *Qu'est-ce que tu n'aimes pas faire?* (What do you not like doing?)

    Je n'aime pas <u>faire les courses</u> et je déteste <u>le tennis</u>.

9   *Qu'est-ce qu'il y a à faire pour les jeunes dans le coin?* (What is there for young people in the area?)

    Il y a <u>une boîte</u> (a nightclub), <u>un centre sportif et une piscine</u>.

10 *Tu aimes ta ville/ton village?* (Do you like your town/village?)

    <u>Non, il n'y a rien à faire</u>. (No, there's nothing to do.)

Sample answers

You can see pupils doing some speaking assessment on the video. Here are a few examples of what you should achieve to get each grade from 1 to 7 (1–2 is a Credit grade, 3–4 is a General grade and 5–7 is a Foundation grade). The three pupils all answer the same questions – but in a different way, so they come out with different grades.

Often you are given a few different topics to speak about. In this example you are asked to introduce yourself to a French friend for the first time, talk about your home area, your school and your hobbies.

T = teacher

T: Tu viens d'où?
  F: ....
  G: Pardon? Je ne comprends pas.
  C: Je suis née à Inverness au nord de l'Ecosse, mais j'habite à Glasgow depuis l'âge de six ans.

T: (changes question for F and G) Où habites-tu?
  F: A Falkirk.
  G: J'habite à Annan. Et toi?

T: J'habite à Soignolles près de Paris.
  C: Qu'est-ce qu'il y a à faire à Soignolles pour les jeunes?

T: Pas grand-chose. Il faut aller à Paris. Qu'est-ce qu'il y a dans ta ville?
  F: Un cinéma, une piscine.
  G: Il y a une patinoire, deux cinémas et des salles de billards américains.
  C: Chez nous, il y a beaucoup de choix. Si on veut, on peut aller au ciné ou en boîte. Si ça t'intéresse, on peut faire des arts martiaux. Qu'est-ce que tu fais pendant tes loisirs?

T: J'adore aller au ciné, s'il y a un bon film. Et toi?
  F: J'adore faire du football.
  G: J'aime faire du sport. Je joue au basket au collège.
  C: Cette année, je passe des examens importants, donc je n'ai pas beaucoup de temps. Mais, en général, je sors avec des copines. On va en boîte.

T: Le collège en Ecosse commence à quelle heure?
  F: ....
  G: A neuf heures. Et en France?
  C: En Ecosse, les cours commencent généralement vers neuf heures moins le quart. Mais c'est très différent en France, n'est-ce pas?

T: (tries to ask the question in different ways for F – unsuccessfully) Tu aimes ton collège?
  F: Non.
  G: Je déteste le collège, à part l'EPS.
  C: Les profs sont sympa, mais il y a quelques matières que je trouve difficiles. J'adore le français parce que le prof est rigolo, mais j'ai horreur des maths.

T = teacher

F = Foundation pupil

G = General pupil

C = Credit pupil

Daily life

! REMEMBER Don't just sit in silence! If you don't understand, say so – in French, of course! In the speaking test, the important thing is to actually say something.

! REMEMBER It's a good idea to ask a few questions yourself – but make sure they're relevant.

! REMEMBER Add as much information as you can – but don't try to say something you're not sure about.

Listening

(TV) You need access to the video to do the listening sections in the book. Your school may have a copy of the video. Why not ask your teacher if you and some friends could watch the video in school and do the exercises from the book. Otherwise the best thing is to tape the programme whenever it is broadcast (check times and dates on Ceefax or the Internet).

(?) Why not revise some vocabulary before you start?

Clémentine's family

(◉) (t/g) (TV) Watch the clip where Clémentine introduces her family. Fill in the details.

Her mother's name:	Chantal	
Her mother's age:		(1)
Her mother's job:		(1)
Her mother's hobby:		(1)
Her brother's name:	Emile	
Her brother's age:		(1)
Number of pets:		(2)
Her father leaves at:		(1)
Her father works at:		(1)
Her father's hobby after work:		(1)

(Total: 9)

! REMEMBER In the exam you will hear each item twice. When you are practising you can listen as often as you like.

! REMEMBER You don't have to understand every word. Listen as carefully as you can.

! REMEMBER If you don't have access to the video, there are some extra listening activities you can do on pages 72–75.

Describing a town

⊙ 🅣 📺   Listen to the people describing their town on the video and complete the adjectives they use. The first two letters are written for you. You can check your answers on the video or at the back of the book. Write beside each adjective what it means in English.

1 ag_____   _____

2 be_____   _____

3 cu_____   _____

4 pe_____   _____

5 tr_____   _____

6 to_____   _____

7 sy_____   _____

8 va_____   _____

9 ga_____   _____

10 vi_____   _____

11 jo_____   _____

12 ca_____   _____

13 ch_____   _____

14 mo_____   _____

15 dy_____   _____

(Total: 30)

> **! REMEMBER**
> Try not to leave blanks, especially in a multiple choice exercise. Your guess could be a lucky one and earn you an extra mark.

Pocket money

⊙ 🅖🅒 📺   What do each of these youngsters say about pocket money?

1 Kony   **(1)**

2 Judith   **(1)**

3 Pejvak   **(1)**

4 Mia   **(1)**

5 Philippe   **(1)**

6 Charlotte   **(1)**

7 Vincent   **(1)**

8 Laure   **(1)**

(Total: 8)

Listening

Favourite subjects

◉ 🄵🄶 🄣🄥 Watch the clip about school life. Beside each person's name write his or her favourite subject.

1 Michael   (1)
_____

2 Mathieu   (1)
_____

3 Julien   (1)
_____

4 Florian   (1)
_____

5 Suldra   (1)
_____

6 Jasmina   (1)
_____

7 Vilma   (1)
_____

8 Ignace   (1)
_____

9 Audrey   (1)
_____

(Total: 9)

❗ REMEMBER Give as many pieces of information as there are marks for each answer.

❗ REMEMBER Always answer questions in English. Any French in an answer might cost you a mark.

Arranging to go out

◉ 🄶🄲 🄣🄥 Clémentine is keen to go out with Patrick. Answer these questions.

1 What does she suggest first of all?   (1)
_____

2 What is his reaction?   (1)
_____

3 Write down three things he likes. (Any three answers.)   (3)
_____

4 When can't he go?   (3)
_____

(Total: 8)

Listening to the radio

◎ f/g TV̈   What do these people say about when or how often they listen to the radio? Tick the right box.

1 *Gladys*   a at night   ☐

                     b at the weekend   ☐

                     c never   ☐

2 *Virginie*   a not as much as she watches TV   ☐

                     b at the weekend   ☐

                     c never   ☐

3 *David*   a not as much as he watches TV   ☐

                     b very often   ☐

                     c never   ☐

4 *Yann*   a when he wakes up   ☐

                     b very often   ☐

                     c at the weekend   ☐

5 *Véronique*   a when she wakes up   ☐

                     b before she goes to bed   ☐

                     c never   ☐

6 *Caroline*   a only at the weekend   ☐

                     b about three hours a day   ☐

                     c about eight hours a week   ☐

7 *Marie-Hélène*   a when she gets up   ☐

                     b before she goes to bed   ☐

                     c only on Sunday mormings   ☐

(Total: 7)

❗ R E M E M B E R
Always read the questions carefully before starting the exercise. They help you to focus on what you need to listen for.

Holidays and travel

This section is about

- Directions
- Hotels and campsites
- Shopping
- Weather

- Travel
- Eating out
- Clothes

! **REMEMBER** In Reading, always answer questions in English. Any French in an answer might cost you a mark.

Reading about directions

◎ *fg* Below are some signs you might come across while in France. Look at them and answer the questions.

Bureau de poste, première à gauche

Interdit de stationner devant l'hôpital

Veuillez ne pas fumer dans les couloirs

Les animaux ne sont pas admis dans notre magasin

Ne pas nourrir les animaux en cage

Le parking gratuit est réservé aux clients du restaurant

Ne jetez pas vos détritus sur la voie publique sous peine d'amende

Salle d'attente, au fond du couloir

1 You want to go to the post office. Where would you go?

2 What are you not allowed to do in front of the hospital?

3 What are you not allowed to do in the corridors?

4 What does this sign say?

5 What are you told not to do?

6 What does this sign say?

7 What might happen to you if you drop litter in the street?

8 Where will you find the waiting room?

(Total: 8)

VocabularyZONE

◉ These phrases will be really useful for your exam, so see if you can try and learn them!

Directions

Tournez à gauche/droite.   Turn left/right.

Allez tout droit.   Straight on.

Par là./Là-bas.   Over there.

Dans le nord/sud/est/ouest.
In the north/south/east/west.

Traversez le pont.   Go across the bridge.

Pour aller à la patinoire, s'il vous plaît?
Could you tell me how to get to
the ice-rink, please?

Je cherche le syndicat d'initiative.
I'm looking for the tourist office.

Travel

en TGV (Train à grande vitesse)
on the High Speed Train

le tunnel sous la Manche
the Channel Tunnel

en mob (short for mobylette)   by moped
(popular amongst French teenagers)

en VTT   by mountain bike

la navette spatiale   the space shuttle

la fusée aérienne   the space rocket

le péage   the toll (where you have to pay)

Hotel and campsite

chambres disponibles   rooms available

avec douche   with a shower

un ascenseur   a lift

un emplacement   a (tent/caravan) pitch

Weather

Refer to expressions given in the Writing
section of this section page 45.

Eating out

la carte   the menu

le plat national   the national dish

le plat du jour   dish of the day

Mon plat préféré est ...
My favourite dish is ...

les entrées/les hors-d'œuvres   the starters

le plat prinicipal   the main course

(un steak) bien cuit   well done (steak)

(un steak) cuit à point   done to a turn

trop cuit   overcooked

pas assez cuit   undercooked

un apéro (apéritif)   a drink (before a meal)

un croque-monsieur
a toasted cheese and ham sandwich

les amuse-gueules   cocktail snacks

une pâtisserie   piece of cake
(or the shop selling them)

Shopping

Ça fait combien?/C'est combien?
How much is it?

C'est tout merci.   That's all, thanks.

les grandes surfaces   large shopping centres

de l'ail   some garlic

un kilo de pommes   a kilo of apples

une livre de fraises   a pound of strawberries

Je peux vous aider?   Can I help you?

Clothes

une cabine d'essayage   a changing room

C'est trop grand/petit.   It's too big/small.

C'est trop cher.   It is too dear.

Je peux essayer ça?   Can I try this on?

BITESIZEfrench

Weather forecast

◎ g/c Read this weather forecast from a French newspaper and fill in the left hand part of each box on the map with the letters below (each letter stands for a kind of weather).

cloudy   A   wind   E

rain   B   snow   F

showers C   sunny G

fog   D

Then write the temperature in the right hand part of each box.

(Total: 14)

Demain, dans le nord de la France, il neigera. Il fera environ 3°C. Dans l'est, il y aura de la pluie en plaine, et les températures seront plus douces : 11°C. Dans la région parisienne, le soleil brillera toute la journée avec des températures atteignant les 13°C. Dans l'ouest, on peut s'attendre à des averses en Bretagne et en Normandie, et il fera froid : 4°C. Dans le centre, du brouillard couvrira les sommets, et les températures pourront descendre jusqu'à 0°C. Dans le sud-ouest, des nuages se développeront tout au long de la journée, et les températures ne dépasseront pas les 15°C. Le sud-est sera très ensoleillé, mais le vent soufflera jusqu'à 80km/h. Voilà pourquoi les températures n'excèderont pas les 16°C.

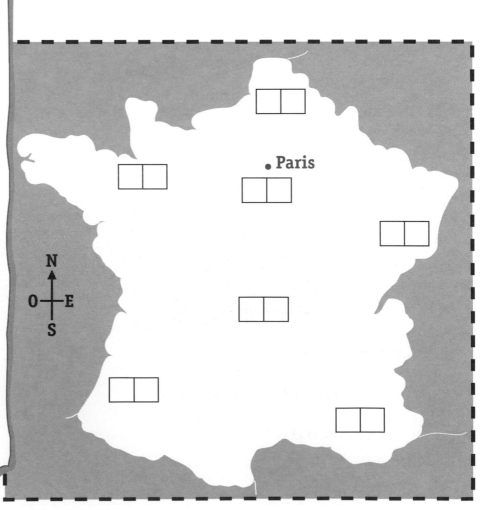

Travel

◎ *f/g*　You have a look at this advert in a travel agent's window.

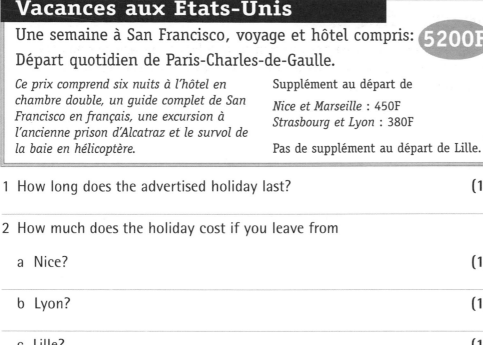

Vacances aux Etats-Unis

Une semaine à San Francisco, voyage et hôtel compris: **5200F**

Départ quotidien de Paris-Charles-de-Gaulle.

Ce prix comprend six nuits à l'hôtel en chambre double, un guide complet de San Francisco en français, une excursion à l'ancienne prison d'Alcatraz et le survol de la baie en hélicoptère.

Supplément au départ de

Nice et Marseille : 450F
Strasbourg et Lyon : 380F

Pas de supplément au départ de Lille.

1　How long does the advertised holiday last? **(1)**

2　How much does the holiday cost if you leave from

　a　Nice? **(1)**

　b　Lyon? **(1)**

　c　Lille? **(1)**

3　How many nights in a hotel does the holiday include? **(1)**

4　What two outings are included in the price? **(2)**

5　How frequent are the flights from Paris? **(1)**

(Total: 8)

REMEMBER Give as many pieces of information as there are marks for each answer.

◎ *g/c*　While on the metro, you read this notice.

– Avertissement aux usagers du métro –
ATTENTION!
La fermeture des portes est automatique. Défense absolue d'ouvrir les portes avant l'arrêt total de la rame en station. Le train ne peut partir que les portes fermées. Ne pas gêner leur fermeture sous peine d'amende. Il est aussi formellement interdit de se pencher au-dehors.

1　What must happen before the metro can leave? **(1)**

2　What is strictly forbidden? Mention two things. **(2)**

3　How do the metro doors close? **(1)**

4　What will happen to travellers not respecting the notice? **(1)**

(Total: 5)

REMEMBER Don't look up every word in the dictionary. First:

• look for words you know

• look for words that look like English words

• underline words that you need to look up to help you answer the questions.

Holidays and travel

Reading

Letter from a hotel

 g/c   Your parents want to spend a few days in France and have sent for information. They received the following letter from a hotel and they ask you to help them to understand it. See if you can help them by answering the questions below.

Hôtel Cheval d'Or
17, rue de la Morée
93270 SEVRAN
Tél. 01.43.84.51.20

Le 23 juillet 1999

Monsieur,

Nous avons bien reçu votre lettre du 15 juillet. Je tiens à vous informer que nous avons des chambres disponibles du 17 au 24 août comme suit : une grande chambre pour deux personnes avec cabinet de toilette, et trois petites chambres à deux lits avec lavabo, toutes les quatres au deuxième étage avec vue sur le canal. Il y a un ascenseur.

Voici nos tarifs pour 1999 :

la grande chambre pour deux personnes	280F par jour
chaque petite chambre pour deux personnes	200F par jour.
Le petit déjeuner est inclus dans nos tarifs.	

L'hôtel se trouve à proximité de la gare SNCF, et l'aéroport n'est qu'à une vingtaine
de minutes en voiture.

En attendant le plaisir de vous lire, veuillez recevoir, Monsieur, l'expression de mes sentiments distingués.

H. Lamaud

H. LAMAUD
Propriétaire, Hôtel Cheval d'Or.

1 From which town was the letter written? **(1)**

2 On which date did your parents write to M. Lamaud? **(1)**

3 What is the period your parents enquired about? **(1)**

4 On which floor of the hotel are the rooms? **(1)**

5 What do the rooms overlook? **(1)**

6 How much would you pay for all three small rooms? **(1)**

7 Is breakfast included? **(1)**

8 How far is the hotel from the airport? **(1)**

(Total: 8)

❗ R E M E M B E R
In General Reading and especially in Credit Reading you're required to give more than just a word or a phrase – give a full answer, but don't add details that are not in the text.

Prepositions

A preposition is often used for saying where someone or something is.

<u>à meaning 'to' or 'at'</u>

masculine singular	feminine singular	before a vowel	plural
au	*à la*	*à l'*	*aux*
j'arrive au café	*tu vas à la Poste*	*il est resté à l'hôtel*	*ils vont aux magasins*

<u>de meaning 'of' or 'from'</u>

masculine singular	feminine singular	before a vowel	plural
du	*de la*	*de l'*	*des*

Some prepositions are followed by **de**, for example:

à côté de   *Il y a un zoo à côté du collège* (masculine).   There is a zoo next to the school.
près de   *Il habite près de l'école* (starts with a vowel).   He lives near the school.
en face de *Le coiffeur est en face de la boulangerie* (feminine).   The hairdresser's is opposite the baker's.

Prepositions with countries and towns

à is used with the names of towns, for example:
   à Dundee   in Dundee/to Dundee
   à Edimbourg   in Edinburgh/to Edinburgh

en is used with the names of countries which are feminine (which are the most common), such as:
   en Ecosse   in Scotland/to Scotland
   en Espagne   in Spain/to Spain

au is used with the names of countries which are masculine, such as:
   au Portugal   in Portugal/to Portugal
   au Brésil   in Brazil/to Brazil

aux is used with plural names, such as:
   aux Pays-Bas   in the Netherlands/to the Netherlands
   aux Etats-Unis   in the USA/to the USA

<u>en with means of transport</u>

As you've seen above, **en** is often used with names of countries and regions. It is also used with most means of transport, such as:
   en bateau   by boat
   en voiture   by car
   en avion   by plane
   en TGV   by high speed train
   en hélicoptère   by helicopter

Holidays and travel

Eating out 1

◎ f/g   You decide to treat yourself and your penfriend. Try to work out this menu and answer the questions.

38

---

restauration rapide : chez Jacques

Ouvert tous les jours sauf mardis

		sur place	à emporter
– demi-baguette :	pâté et saucisson	30F	27F
	poulet, tomate, salade	32F	29F
– pizza :	fromage et jambon	26F	24F
	champignons et lardons	34F	32F
– croque-monsieur :		24F	22F

+ une barquette de frites comprise dans nos prix!

| – boisson (Coca, Fanta, Perrier, eau minérale 50cl) | 10F | 10F |

Bon appétit !

---

1 When is the restaurant open? (1)

2 How much would it cost you for a half baguette with chicken, tomato and lettuce to take away? (1)

3 How much is it for a cheese and ham pizza if you sit in? (1)

4 What is included in all the prices? (1)

5 How much is it for a mineral water? (1)

(Total: 5)

Making comparisons

To compare one person or thing with another, you use **plus** (more), **moins** (less) or **aussi** (as) before the adjective and **que** (or **qu'**) after it.

Elle est plus belle que toi.   She is more beautiful than you.

Tu es moins bête que lui.   You are less stupid than him.

Je cours aussi vite que toi.   I run as fast as you.

Note that there are two exceptions to learn:

bon (good) ⇨ *meilleur* (better)

mauvais (bad) ⇨ *pire* (worse)

L'eau est meilleure que le vin.   Water is better than wine.

Son caractère est pire que le mien.   His temper is worse than mine.

The superlative

To say that something is the best, fastest, longest, greatest etc. you use the superlative.

Paul est le plus petit de sa classe.   Paul is the smallest in his class.

Londres est la plus grande ville d'Angleterre.   London is the biggest town in England.

C'est le pire restaurant d'Inverness.   It's the worst restaurant in Inverness.

Note that you use **le**, **la** or **les** and the correct ending of the adjective, depending on whether the noun is masculine, feminine or plural.

If the adjective normally comes after the noun, the superlative will also follow the noun (see examples above). If the adjective normally comes before the noun, the superlative does too:

l'avion le plus rapide   the fastest plane

la plus petite voiture   the smallest car

'Very', 'quite', 'too' + adjective

Tu es très belle.   You are very beautiful.

Elle est assez grande.   She is quite tall.

Nous sommes trop impatients.   We are too impatient.

Holidays and travel

Reading

Eating out 2

◎ *flg*   You read this leaflet introducing a restaurant near your penfriend's home.

Chez Florian

paëlla   **couscous**

Florian vous accueille dans son restaurant au cadre moderne (sur deux étages), 2 avenue Eugène Schueller à Aulnay-sous-Bois.

❖

Notre entrée se présente sous la forme d'un copieux buffet où on se sert à volonté.

❖

Vous pouvez ensuite déguster nos spécialités grecques (sandwichs, grillades), algériennes (couscous), espagnoles (paëlla) et françaises (cassoulet, fondue savoyarde).

❖

Nos desserts glacés sont réputés pour leurs saveurs succulentes et nos pâtisseries sont faites maison.

Nos prix sont aussi abordables, à partir de 110F (pour une entrée, un plat, et un dessert au choix).

grillades   **cassoulet**

Bon appétit et à bientôt!

> **REMEMBER**
> Don't be too surprised when you don't find every single word in the dictionary. To include every word, it would be huge.

> **REMEMBER**
> Give as many pieces of information as there are marks for each answer.

1 What does the starter consist of?   (1)

2 What countries do the dishes originate from? Mention any three.   (3)

3 What is home-made?   (1)

4 What are their puddings famous for?   (1)

5 What do you get for 110F?   (3)

(Total: 9)

At the supermarket

◎ *flg*   While in France your penfriend's mother asks you to go and do her shopping as she is not well. What supermarket aisles will you have to find? Match the food items on the left with the supermarket sections on the right. Write the letter of the supermarket section (A–H) next to the item on the shopping list.

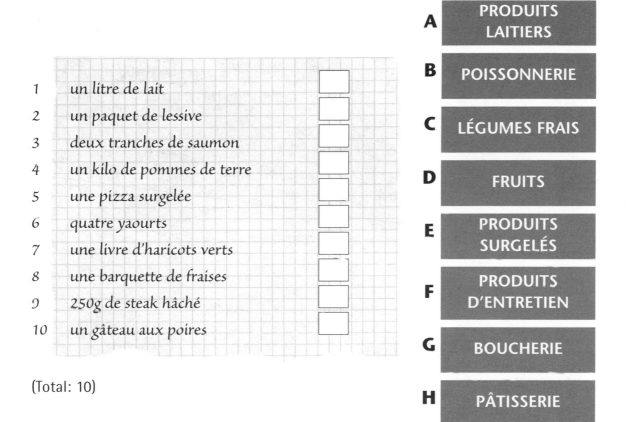

1   un litre de lait

2   un paquet de lessive

3   deux tranches de saumon

4   un kilo de pommes de terre

5   une pizza surgelée

6   quatre yaourts

7   une livre d'haricots verts

8   une barquette de fraises

9   250g de steak haché

10 un gâteau aux poires

(Total: 10)

A PRODUITS LAITIERS

B POISSONNERIE

C LÉGUMES FRAIS

D FRUITS

E PRODUITS SURGELÉS

F PRODUITS D'ENTRETIEN

G BOUCHERIE

H PÂTISSERIE

Holidays and travel

◎ *flg*   **Trouve l'intrus.** Circle the odd one out.

1 **Food:** une pomme de terre, un jus de pomme, une poire, un ananas

2 **Travel:** un avion, un ballon dirigeable, une navette spatiale, un bateau

3 **Hotel, campsite:** un emplacement de tente, un hôtel deux étoiles, service compris, une auberge de jeunesse

4 **Clothes:** un chemisier, une chemise, une cravate, un caleçon

5 **Directions:** tout droit, tournez à droite, droit devant vous, ne tournez pas

❗ REMEMBER Try not to leave blanks, especially in a multiple choice exercise. Your guess could be a lucky one and earn you an extra mark.

Reading

Clothes

 While at your penfriend's, you have a look at this leaflet advertising articles of clothing on sale in a shop.

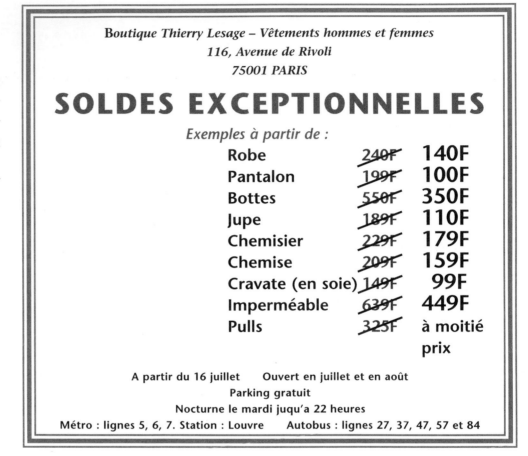

Boutique Thierry Lesage – Vêtements hommes et femmes
116, Avenue de Rivoli
75001 PARIS

SOLDES EXCEPTIONNELLES

Exemples à partir de :

Robe	~~240F~~	**140F**
Pantalon	~~199F~~	**100F**
Bottes	~~550F~~	**350F**
Jupe	~~189F~~	**110F**
Chemisier	~~229F~~	**179F**
Chemise	~~209F~~	**159F**
Cravate (en soie)	~~149F~~	**99F**
Imperméable	~~639F~~	**449F**
Pulls	~~325F~~	**à moitié prix**

A partir du 16 juillet   Ouvert en juillet et en août
Parking gratuit
Nocturne le mardi juqu'a 22 heures
Métro : lignes 5, 6, 7. Station : Louvre   Autobus : lignes 27, 37, 47, 57 et 84

1 What articles are in the sale? Mention any five. (5)

2 Does this store sell (1)
  a men's clothing only?   b women's clothing only?   c both?

3 By how much has the price of skirts been reduced? (1)

4 When do the sales start? (1)

5 Which is the nearest underground station to the shop? (1)

6 What happens on Tuesdays? (1)

(Total: 10)

REMEMBER Don't just use your general knowledge or common sense. Look carefully at the French.

REMEMBER In question 1 you're asked for five pieces of information and there are many more in the text. Choose the five you know best. If you write too much, you may lose marks.

42

Subject pronouns

Pronouns are words which stand in for the name of a person or thing.

je	I
tu	you (informal singular)
il/elle	he/she/it
nous	we
vous	you (polite or plural)
ils/elles	they

In French, **on** is also used. In English, **on** can mean 'one', 'you', 'they' or 'we' depending on the context.

> *On va au cinéma?*   Shall we go to the cinema?

Verbs

The tense of the verb tells you when the action took place, for example:

> *J'écoute de la musique.* (present tense)   I listen/am listening to music.

> *J'ai écouté de la musique.* (perfect tense)   I (have) listened to music.

Verbs – the infinitive

If you look for a verb in the dictionary or a vocabulary list, it will be given in the form called the infinitive, such as:

> *écouter*   to listen   *attendre*   to wait   *rougir*   to blush

There are three main groups of verbs in French:

- verbs which end in **-er** in the infinitive (e.g. **écouter**)

- verbs which end in **-ir** in the infinitive (e.g. **rougir**)

- verbs which end in **-re** in the infinitive (e.g. **attendre**)

Verbs + **à** + infinitive

Some verbs are followed by **à** + the infinitive of a second verb, such as:

> *apprendre à*   *Il apprend à parler anglais.*   He is learning to speak English.

> *commencer à*   *Il a commencé à faire ses valises.*   He started to pack his suitcase.

> *demander à*   *Il a demandé à rentrer plus tôt.*   He asked to go home early.

Verbs + **de** + infinitive

Some verbs are followed by **de** + the infinitive of a second verb, such as:

> *décider de*   *Nous avons décidé de sortir.*   We decided to go out.

> *refuser de*   *Vous refusez de coopérer?*   Are you refusing to cooperate?

> *oublier de*   *J'ai oublié de fermer le gaz.*   I forgot to turn off the gas.

Holidays and travel

Making a very simple essay more complicated

- Most of the time you write in the present tense, so check your knowledge of the present tense. (See **GrammarZONE** page 47.)

- You can just use the **je** form of the verb and add other people on odd occasions. You'll be shown how to do that.

- You can use the same expressions in different essays – most of the time. Below is a simple essay for you. It's about what you do on holiday – but you can transfer some of the expressions and sentences to other essays, such as those about the weekend, shopping, daily routine, pocket money etc.

Simple essay

Here's the simple essay. You'll notice it is almost 100 words long (i.e. half the length your essay is supposed to be). In the **VocabularyZONE** (opposite) is a list of the kind of things you can add to make a full essay.

Je me lève à dix heures. Je prends le petit déjeuner. Je mange des fruits et je bois du jus d'orange. Je prends une douche. Je m'habille. Je quitte l'hôtel. Je vais à la plage. Je prends le déjeuner. Je fais les magasins. Ma sœur cherche des souvenirs. Je regarde des magazines. On boit un café. On mange un gâteau. On rentre à l'hôtel. On dîne à huit heures. Je regarde la télé. Je joue au baby-foot. Je mange un bol de céréales. Je me couche.

In the answer section at the back of this book you will find a more complicated essay based on this simple essay but with some of the expressions in the **VocabularyZONE** (opposite) added on.

 Below is a short paragraph about a **past** holiday. To keep it simple, just write about your own holiday following the same pattern.

Je suis allé(e) à Marseille en vacances. J'ai voyagé en train. Je suis resté(e) deux semaines. J'ai loué une chambre d'hôtel. J'ai rencontré des jeunes de mon âge. J'ai visité la ville. J'ai fait les magasins. J'ai acheté des souvenirs. Il a fait beau. Je me suis bronzé(e). Je suis allé(e) au cinéma. J'ai regardé un film.

This is approximatively 60 words. Just by adding other expressions or joining words from the **VocabularyZONE** (opposite), this could be doubled! Try to re-write it by adding some of them.

---

44 **!** **REMEMBER** This is a BITESIZE book, not a banquet – not all the vocabulary is included. You also have to refer to your notes from school.

! **REMEMBER** Try not to use the dictionary. If you have to, just look up a few words that you've forgotten. If you don't know an expression, don't use it! You can't write an essay (not even a sentence) from a dictionary.

Joining words

et – and   donc – therefore   mais – but

où – where   lorsque – when   si – if

puis – then   parce que – because

Places

chez moi, à la maison   at home/to my house

à la plage   to/at the beach

chez mon frère   to/at my brother's

en ville   to/in town

en Grèce   to/in Greece

au collège   to/at school

près de   near

à côté de   next to

loin de   far from

Time expressions

le matin   in the morning

le midi   at lunchtime

l'après-midi   in the aftenoon

le soir   in the evening

vers deux heures et demie   at about 2.30

lundi   this Monday, on Monday, next Monday

le lundi   on Mondays

après avoir pris le petit déjeuner
   after having breakfast

avant de me coucher   before going to bed

quand il fait beau   when the weather is nice

souvent   often

parfois   sometimes

enfin   at last

quand j'ai le temps   when I have time

après le collège   after school

People

avec mes copains   with my friends (boys
   only or boys and girls)

avec mes copines   with my friends (girls only)

avec mon copain   with my (boy)friend

avec ma copine   with my (girl)friend

tout(e) seul(e)   on my own

en famille   with the family

Reasons

parce que j'aime la cuisine italienne
   because I like Italian food

parce qu'il fait beau   because the weather's nice

pour voir mes amis   to see my friends

pour acheter des souvenirs   to buy souvenirs

Weather expressions

Il fait beau.   It's nice weather.

Il fait du soleil.   It's sunny.

Il fait froid.   It's cold.

Il fait chaud.   It's hot.

Il fait frais.   It's chilly.

Il ne fait pas très chaud.   It's not very warm.

Il pleut.   It's raining./It rains.

C'est nuageux./Il fait gris.   It's cloudy.

Il fait doux.   It's mild.

Time expressions with the past tense

le lendemain   the next day

pendant les grandes vacances
   during the summer holidays

pendant les vacances de Pâques
   during the Easter holidays

l'année dernière   last year

la semaine d'après   the following week

Writing

A postcard from your holidays

◉ *f/g* Fill in the blanks on this postcard by choosing one word or expression from each box according to the number shown. Don't forget to sign it!

46

❗ REMEMBER
Always take time to read your answers again at the end to see if they really make sense.

Chère Sophie,

Je suis en vacances à (1)_____.

Je suis arrivé (arrivée if you are a girl)

(2)_____.

C'est super ici!

(3)_____.

Tous les jours, je (4)_____.

Le matin, je me lève à

(5)_____. Le soir, je me

couche à (5)_____.

A bientot.

_____

1   Paris   Toulouse   Bordeaux

2   lundi (Monday)   mardi (Tuesday)   mercredi (Wednesday)   jeudi (Thursday)   vendredi (Friday)   samedi (Saturday)   dimanche

3   il fait beau   il fait chaud   il pleut
(see Weather expressions on page 45)

4   vais à la plage (go to the beach)   visite des musées (visit museums)   fais du lèche-vitrine (go window-shopping)   joue

5   six heures   neuf heures   midi   deux heures

(Total: 6)

Verbs – the present tense

The present tense describes what someone is doing at the moment or does regularly.

Regular verbs

The usual pattern of each of the three main groups of verbs is as follows. Verbs which follow this pattern are called regular verbs.

	écouter (to listen)	*rougir* (to blush)	*attendre* (to wait)
I	*j'écoute*	*je rougis*	*j'attends*
you (informal)	*tu écoutes*	*tu rougis*	*tu attends*
he/she/it/one	*il/elle/on écoute*	*il/elle/on rougit*	*il/elle/on attend*
we	*nous écoutons*	*nous rougissons*	*nous attendons*
you (formal/plural)	*vous écoutez*	*vous rougissez*	*vous attendez*
they	*ils/elles écoutent*	*ils/elles rougissent*	*ils/elles attendent*

Irregular verbs

Verbs which do not follow the above patterns are called irregular verbs. Here are some of the most common ones.

être (to be)	*avoir* (to have)	*aller* (to go)	*faire* (to do, make)
je suis	*j'ai*	*je vais*	*je fais*
tu es	*tu as*	*tu vas*	*tu fais*
il/elle/on est	*il/elle/on a*	*il/elle/on va*	*il/elle/on fait*
nous sommes	*nous avons*	*nous allons*	*nous faisons*
vous êtes	*vous avez*	*vous allez*	*vous faites*
ils/elles sont	*ils/elles ont*	*ils/elles vont*	*ils/elles font*

Reflexive verbs

Reflexive verbs are used to give the idea of 'myself', 'yourself', 'himself', 'herself' etc. You need to use an extra reflexive pronoun – **me, te, se, nous, vous** – with these verbs.

Here are some common reflexive verbs.

s'habiller	to get dressed
se lever	to get up
se coucher	to go to bed
s'asseoir	to sit down

In the present tense, the reflexive forms are as follows:

je me lève	I get up
tu te lèves	you get up
il/elle/on se lève	he/she/one gets up
nous nous levons	we get up
vous vous levez	you get up
ils se lèvent	they get up

● ●●● Speaking

Holidays 1

48

! REMEMBER
Try to give more than just a one word answer.

Use some of the simple phrases from the essays in the Writing section to prepare a talk on your holiday.

Then add some of the other words and expressions given in the **VocabularyZONE** (page 45). Remember – the more you can say, the better your chances of a better grade.

Here are some questions you might be asked.

1 *Tu pars en vacances ou tu restes à la maison?* (Do you go on holiday or do you stay home?)

2 *Qu'est-ce que tu fais pendant les vacances?* (What do you do during the holidays?)

3 *Comment est-ce que tu voyages?* (How do you travel?)

4 *Tu pars en famille?* (Do you go with your family?)

5 *Où vas-tu en vacances?* (Where do you go on holiday?)

6 *Où est-ce que tu loges?* (Where do you stay?)

7 *Pourquoi est-ce que tu y vas?* (Why do you go there?)

8 *Qu'est-ce qu'il y a à faire là-bas pour les jeunes?* (What is there to do for young people over there?)

9 *Tu te lèves à quelle heure en vacances?* (What time do you get up on holiday?)

10 *Tu te couches à quelle heure en vacances?* (What time do you go to bed during the holidays?)

11 *Quelles sont les spécialités de la région?* (What are the traditional regional dishes?)

12 *Qu'est-ce qu'on peut visiter?* (What is there to visit?)

If you don't go on holiday, you can still say lots of things or make it up. Nobody will go and check if it's true or not! If you do stay at home, here are some of the things you can say.

1 *Je reste à la maison.* (I stay at home.)

2 Say what you do.

Je vais en ville (I go to town), *je fais de la natation* (I go swimming), *je vais chez des copains* (I go and visit my friends).

3 Mention local trips you go on.

Je vais à la plage (I go to the beach), *je vais au Loch Ness* (I go to Loch Ness), *je visite le musée* (I visit the museum).

Possessive adjectives

In French there are different words for 'my', 'your' etc. It depends whether the word they belong with is masculine (m), feminine (f) or plural (pl).

	m	f	pl
my	mon	ma	mes
your (familiar)	ton	ta	tes
his	son	sa	ses
her	son	sa	ses
our	notre	notre	nos
your (plural and polite)	votre	votre	vos
their	leur	leur	leurs

Note: if a feminine word begins with a vowel you always use the masculine form (e.g. *mon amie*).

A letter from Béatrice

◎ Read this letter in which a Belgian girl introduces herself. Fill in the gaps with the French for the words in brackets. The glossary below reminds you if the words are masculine or feminine. Remember, plural words usually end in *-s* or *-x*.

Chère Marie,

Merci de ____ (your) lettre. Je m'appelle Béatrice. Je suis belge. J'ai treize ans. ____ (My) père est prof de mathématiques et ____ (my) mère est comptable. ___ (My) parents sont divorcés. ____ (My) père s'est remarié et il habite avec ____ (his) femme et _____ (their) deux enfants en France. _____ (Our) appartement est à Bruxelles en Belgique. J'ai deux frères. ____ (My) frère aîné est étudiant en France et ____ (my) petit frère, qui a quatre ans, va à l'école maternelle. ____ (His) école se trouve à deux kilomètres de chez nous.

Tu as dit que tu as deux sœurs et un frère. Comment s'appellent-elles, ____ (your) deux sœurs ? ____ (Your) frère, quel âge a-t-il ? Combien de pièces y a-t-il dans ____ (your) maison ? Est-ce que ____ (your) collège est près de chez toi ?

Ecris vite.

Béatrice

maison (f)	collège (m)	mère (f)
appartement (m)	école (f)	père (m)
enfant (m/f)	femme (f)	parent (m/f)
frère (m)	lettre (f)	sœur (f)

Speaking

Holidays 2

REMEMBER
Usually answer in the tense of the question.

Answer these questions about your holidays. Use the words and phrases below to help you, and add some of your own.

1 *Où vas-tu en vacances?*
(Where do you go on holiday?)
Je reste …
   à la maison
   en Ecosse
   à (+ name of your town or village)
Je vais …
   en Angleterre
   en Espagne
   en France
   à (+ name of town or village)

2 *Tu pars avec qui?*
(Who do you go with?)
Je pars …
   en famille
   avec ma sœur
   tout(e) seul(e)
Je reste … (see question 1)

3 *Qu'est-ce que tu fais en vacances?*
(What do you do on holiday?)
Je joue …
   au foot
   avec mes copains
   au baby-foot
Je fais …
   les magasins
   du sport
   de la natation

4 *Où vas-tu pendant les vacances?*
(Where do you go during the holidays?)
Je vais …
   à la plage
   en ville
   au ciné

5 *Tu te lèves à quelle heure?*
(What time do you get up?)
Je me lève à …
   dix heures
   onze heures
   midi

6 *A quelle heure est-ce que tu te couches?*
(When do you go to bed?)
Je me couche à …
   minuit
   une heure du matin
   trois heures

7 *Qu'est-ce que tu manges et qu'est-ce que tu bois?*
(What do you eat and drink?)
Je mange …
   les spécialités de la région
   des frites
   beaucoup de fruits
Je bois …
   du coca
   du vin
   toutes sortes de choses

8 *Quel temps fait-il en été?*
(What's the weather like in summer?)
Il …
   pleut
   fait beau
   fait chaud

9 *Qu'est-ce que tu achètes comme souvenirs?*
(What souvenirs do you buy?)
J'achète …
   des bonbons
   des posters
   du vin

10 *Quel est ton pays préféré?*
(What's your favourite country?)
Mon pays préféré est …
   l'Allemagne
   les Etats-Unis
   l'Ecosse

Modal verbs

This is the name given to a group of verbs which can be added to a sentence with another verb in the infinitive, such as:

En France, on doit conduire à gauche. In France you must drive on the right.

Vous pouvez répéter? Can you repeat that?

Here are the present tense forms of four common modal verbs.

pouvoir	*vouloir*	*devoir*	*savoir*
(to be able to/can)	(to want)	(to have to/must)	(to know how to)
je peux	*je veux*	*je dois*	*je sais*
tu peux	*tu veux*	*tu dois*	*tu sais*
il/elle/on peut	*il/elle/on veut*	*il/elle/on doit*	*il/elle/on sait*
nous pouvons	*nous voulons*	*nous devons*	*nous savons*
vous pouvez	*vous voulez*	*vous devez*	*vous savez*
ils/elles peuvent	*ils/elles veulent*	*ils/elles doivent*	*ils/elles savent*

Verbs – the future tense

The future tense describes what someone will do or is going to do. There are three ways in French of talking about the future, but for your exam two of them (the easiest and most common ones) will do.

• You can simply use the present tense of the verb **aller** (to go) + any infinitive, for example:

Je vais apprendre le français. I'm going to learn French.

Nous allons partir en vacances We're going to go on holiday.

• Easier still, you can use the present tense to talk about the future if you add some expressions of time, for example:

Demain, je prends l'avion. Tomorrow I'm taking the plane.

L'année prochaine, je pars en vacances en Egypte. Next year I'm going on holiday to Egypt.

51

Holidays and travel

Listening

Hotel Canella Beach

◎ ⓖ/ⓒ ⓣⓥ Listen to the video clip where the voice speaks over a list on the screen like the one below. Fill in the details.

Number of bedrooms: (1)

Location of hotel: (1)

Breakfast menu: (5)

Facilities: (7)

(Total: 14)

REMEMBER If you don't have access to the video, there are some extra listening activities you can do on pages 72–75.

REMEMBER Leave plenty of space in your answers so you can go back and change them or fill in any missing details. Write as much information as you can.

Booking a room

◎ ⓖ/ⓒ ⓣⓥ Look at the clip where the businessman is booking a room from his car phone. Fill in the blanks.

REMEMBER You can listen as often as you like.

> He wants a room booked for _____ nights,
> from _____ to _____ .
> He wants a room with a _____ .
> Breakfast costs _____ .
> His name is spelt _____ .

(Total: 6)

Numbers

(?) For the next exercise, you will need to revise your numbers. You need to know the numbers below. You can work out all the rest from these.

0 zéro

1	un	11	onze	30	trente
2	deux	12	douze	40	quarante
3	trois	13	treize	50	cinquante
4	quatre	14	quatorze	60	soixante
5	cinq	15	quinze	70	soixante-dix
6	six	16	seize	80	quatre-vingts
7	sept	17	dix-sept	90	quatre-vingt-dix
8	huit	18	dix-huit	100	cent
9	neuf	19	dix-neuf		
10	dix	20	vingt	1000	mille

Statistics

◎ 🆃🅶 📺 Watch the clip about the TGV and fill in the statistics.

REMEMBER
Always read the questions carefully before starting the exercise. They help you to focus on what you need to listen for.

1 Cost from Paris – Le Mans _____ _____ francs

2 Number of carriages: _____

3 Number of First Class seats: _____

4 Number of Second Class seats: _____

5 Total number of passengers per day: _____

6 Number of return trips per day: _____

7 Normal speed: _____

8 Time from Paris – Le _____ Mans
minutes

(Total: 8)

Holidays and travel

! REMEMBER Try not to leave blanks, especially in a multiple choice exercise. Your guess could be a lucky one and earn you an extra mark.

Travelling by train

◎ g/c TV Watch the clip and tick the correct answer.

1 Departure time

    a 8.35 ☐

    b 9.20 ☐

2 Class of ticket

    a 1st ☐

    b 2nd ☐

3 Number of people

    a 1 ☐

    b 2 ☐

4 Type of seat

    a window seat ☐

    b aisle seat ☐

5 Type of ticket

    a single ☐

    b return ☐

6 Price

    a 246 F ☐

    b 24,60 F ☐

(Total: 6)

Going on holiday

◎ g/c TV Watch the video clip where Clémentine is discussing holidays with her parents. Tick the correct answer.

1 What does Clémentine say to her parents? **(1)**

    a I don't want to go on holiday this year. ☐

    b I don't want to go on holiday with you. ☐

    c I don't want to stay at home this summer. ☐

2 Where does she want to go? **(1)**

    a Italy ☐

    b Germany ☐

    c Tunisia ☐

3 How does she intend to get there? **(1)**

    a by coach ☐

    b hitch-hiking ☐

    c by train ☐

4 Where does she intend to stay at night? **(1)**

    a youth hostel ☐

    b hotel ☐

    c campsite ☐

5 Who does she intend to go with? (1)

  a her sister ☐

  b her boyfriend ☐

  c her cousin ☐

6 What do her parents answer? (1)

  a No way! ☐

  b Maybe. ☐

  c Only if you're sensible. ☐

(Total: 6)

Shopping

◉ *f/g* 📺   Look at the clip where a woman is shopping for vegetables at the market. The shopping list below is not quite accurate. Change it where necessary.

(Total: 3)

> Liste d'achats
> 2–3 aubergines
> 200g courgettes
> 1/2 kg de tomates
> 3 pommes de terre
> de l'ail

Clothes

◉ *f/g* 📺 What do the following people like wearing? Write as many details as you can.

Florent (2)

_____

Vincent (3)

_____

David (1)

_____

Caroline (5)

_____

Marie-Hélène (2)

_____

Frédéric (1)

_____

(Total: 14)

Holidays and travel

Teenage concerns

This section is about

- The world of work
- The environment
- Healthy living
- People and personal relationships

Reading about people and relationships

◎ g/c   Read this magazine article and answer the questions below.

 REMEMBER You are allowed to use a dictionary in the reading exams. It's best to have your own so that you know how it's organised. Check with your school which they recommend.

La vie de Diana

Diana Frances Spencer est née en 1961 à Sandringham dans le sud de l'Angleterre. A seize ans, elle quitte l'école et devient puéricultrice (elle s'occupe de bébés). Puis à dix-neuf ans, elle se marie avec le Prince Charles. Le 21 juin 1982 naît son premier fils : William. Puis en 1984, un deuxième fils, Harry. Ensuite, le 9 décembre 1992, le Prince Charles et Diana annoncent leur séparation au monde entier. Le 28 août 1996, le couple divorce. Diana reste malgré tout la reine du cœur pour des milliers de gens. Elle court d'hôpitaux en associations pour aider ceux qui en ont besoin. Les malades, les pauvres, les enfants, les victimes de guerre ... Elle voyage à travers le monde pour leur porter secours, les écouter ... jusqu'à ce fameux 31 août ou un accident met fin à sa vie à l'âge de trente-six ans.

 REMEMBER Don't just use your general knowledge or common sense. Look carefully at the French.

1 In which part of Britain was Diana born? Tick the right box. **(1)**

in the north ☐

in the south ☐

in the north east ☐

2 When did she leave school? **(1)**

_____

3 What was her first job? **(1)**

_____

4 Why was the 21st of June an important date for her? **(1)**

_____

5 What happened on the 28th of August 1996? **(1)**

_____

6 The article mentions four kinds of people she helped. Name three. **(3)**

_____

(Total: 8)

Verbs – the perfect tense

The perfect tense is used to talk about events which have happened in the past.

Choice of avoir or être

There are two parts of the perfect tense: the auxiliary verb (which is always part of either *avoir* or *être*) and the past participle of a verb.

   J'ai accepté ce travail.   I accepted the work.
   Vous avez commandé?   Have you ordered?
   Je suis parti à quatre heures.   I left at four o'clock.
   Nous sommes venus ensemble.   We came together.

Note: there are 13 verbs, mostly verbs of movement, that form the perfect tense with *être*.
   entrer (to enter)   *sortir* (to go out)   *arriver* (to arrive) *partir* (to leave)
   monter (to go up) *descendre* (to go down) *aller* (to go)   *venir* (to come)
   rester (to stay)   *retourner* (to go back)   *naître* (to be born) *mourir* (to die) *tomber* (to fall)
   Verbs which include *venir* (e.g. *revenir, devenir*) also form the perfect tense with *être*.

Past participle of regular verbs

To make the past participle of a regular verb use the following patterns.
-**er** verbs   The **-er** changes to **-é**.   *écouter* ⇨ *écouté*
-**ir** verbs   The **-ir** changes to **-i**.   *rougir* ⇨ *rougi*
-**re** verbs   The **-re** changes to **-u**.   *attendre* ⇨ *attendu*
Here are some examples.

Verbs with **avoir**:
   Hier, j'ai commencé un livre.   Yesterday I started a book.
   Quand j'ai vu Corinne, j'ai rougi.   When I saw Corinne, I blushed.
   Ils ont entendu le bruit.   They heard the noise.
Verbs with **être**:
   L'année dernière, je suis retourné en Italie.   Last year I went back to Italy.
   Ils sont restés chez eux.   They stayed home.
   Vous êtes sortis hier matin?   Did you go out yesterday morning?

Note: for verbs which take **être**, the past participle agrees with the subject of the verb. No ending is added for the masculine singular, but you add **-e** for feminine and **-s** for plural.
   il est parti – elle est partie   *ils sont retournés – elles sont retournées*

Reflexive verbs

Reflexive verbs also form the perfect tense with **être**. As with other verbs which form the perfect tense with **être**, the past participle agrees with the subject of the verb.
   Je me suis lavé.   I got washed. (if it's a boy speaking)
   Je me suis levée.   I got up. (if it's a girl speaking)
   Elles se sont réveillées.   They (girls) woke up.

! REMEMBER Always read the introduction to the passage.

Racial prejudice

◎ **f/g** You learn languages to be able to meet other people and communicate with them as well as to discover new customs. This should put an end to any prejudice you may have had. Read this text and write down any <u>seven</u> items mentioned and where they come from. Then work out what the last sentence means.

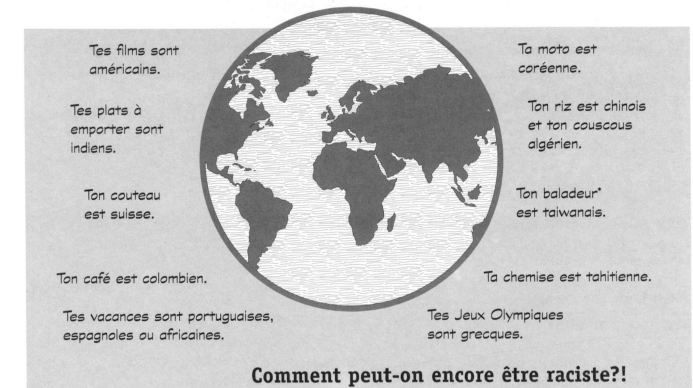

Tes films sont américains.

Tes plats à emporter sont indiens.

Ton couteau est suisse.

Ton café est colombien.

Tes vacances sont portuguaises, espagnoles ou africaines.

Ta moto est coréenne.

Ton riz est chinois et ton couscous algérien.

Ton baladeur* est taiwanais.

Ta chemise est tahitienne.

Tes Jeux Olympiques sont grecques.

Comment peut-on encore être raciste?!

*baladeur**
personal stereo

item	where from	
		(2)
		(2)
		(2)
		(2)
		(2)
		(2)
		(2)

The question at the end means: (1)

(Total: 15)

The world of work 1

◎ ⑨ⓒ This is an article made after interviewing a popular journalist.

Un présentateur sportif

A douze ans, il était fier de porter le célèbre maillot blanc et bleu du Racing Club de France. « J'étais un problème pour mes professeurs, car j'étais chahuteur mais aussi travailleur, toujours premier en gym, et souvent en tête pour les autres matières. » Après avoir voulu être médecin – « le désir de réparer les autres » – il a le coup de foudre pour le journalisme à dix-huit ans en assistant aux informations de la radio *Europe 1*. « Depuis dix ans que je suis au service des sports, je n'ai jamais connu une période aussi chargée, avec les Coupes d'Europe de foot, Roland Garros, les Jeux Olympiques, le Tour de France ... » Le vélo ! Depuis une petite blessure au foot, il l'a adopté. Il participe même à des courses avec des amis. Pendant le tournoi de tennis de Roland Garros, Gérard Holtz suivra les matches et présentera tous les soirs, sauf le mardi, le résumé des matches de la journée, vers 22h15.

59

! R E M E M B E R
Always read the questions carefully before starting the exercise. They help you to focus on what you need to look for.

! R E M E M B E R
Always take time to read your answers again at the end. Make sure your answers make sense.

1 In what ways was this journalist:

  a a delight for his teachers? (1)

  b infuriating? (1)

2 What job did he first want to do? Why? (2)

3 At what age did he become interested in journalism? Tick the right box. (1)

  10 years old ☐

  18 years old ☐

  20 years old ☐

4 How long has he been a sports reporter? (1)

5 Why did he go on to cycling instead of football? (1)

6 On what days will he present a summary of the Roland Garros tennis open? (1)

(Total: 8)

Teenage concerns

The environment

◎ *f/g*   Some of the statements or words below are bad news for the environment or your health. Some others sound better. Separate them into two groups by ticking the positive or negative box. Then give their English equivalent.

! REMEMBER Try not to leave blanks. Your guess could be a lucky one and earn you an extra mark.

		+	**−**	**English**
1	la pollution			
2	le nucléaire			
3	l'essence sans plomb			
4	l'effet de serre			
5	ne contient pas de CFC			
6	les produits chimiques			
7	préserve la couche d'ozone			
8	gaz d'échappement			
9	sans colorant ni conservateur			
10	insecticide			

(Total: 20)

◎ *f/g*   Find these words in French in the wordsearch below (use a dictionary if you need to): battery, acid, camcorder, pollution, recycling, waste, ozone, rubbish, lead, doping.

R	A	S	A	R	D	O	P	P	D
O	C	A	M	E	S	C	O	P	E
P	I	L	E	C	O	D	L	U	C
L	D	S	B	Y	R	O	L	Z	H
O	E	A	A	C	D	P	U	R	E
M	G	J	F	L	U	A	T	N	T
B	H	L	I	A	R	G	I	Q	S
E	M	O	K	G	E	E	O	C	Q
O	Z	O	N	E	S	R	N	P	D

VocabularyZONE

◎ These phrases will be really useful for your exam, so see if you can try and learn them!

The environment

la pluie acide   acid rain

le tapage nocturne   noise at night

la marée noire   oil slick

les déchets nucléaires   nuclear waste

un site contaminé   a contaminated site

des produits biodégradables
   biodegradable products

le dépérissement de la forêt
   decline of the forest

pour protéger la nature
   to protect the environment

on devrait   one should

utiliser l'essence sans plomb
   use unleaded petrol

recycler le verre   recycle glass

faire le tri des déchets domestiques
   sort household rubbish

acheter des piles rechargeables
   buy rechargeable batteries

Je suis contre l'exploitation animal.
   I am against animal exploitation.

Je suis pour l'arrêt des essais nucléaires.
   I am for the end of nuclear tests.

Healthy living

un régime amincissant   a slimming diet

C'est bon pour la forme.
   It's good for your figure.

le SIDA   AIDS

la maladie   illness

la santé   health

les préservatifs   condoms

les serviettes hygiéniques   sanitary towels

un papier mouchoir/un kleenex   a paper hanky

J'ai mal à la tête.   I have a sore head.

J'ai mal au ventre.   I have a sore stomach.

J'ai mal aux oreilles.   I have sore ears.

People and personal relationships

un SDF (Sans Domicile Fixe)   person of no
   fixed abode, homeless person

Il est sans famille.   He hasn't got a family.

généreux/généreuse   generous

sensible   sensitive

travailleur/travailleuse   hard-working

sportif/sportive   fond of sport

agressif/agressive   aggressive

drôle, rigolo/rigolote   funny

gentil/gentille   kind

méchant/méchante   wicked

timide   shy

Je m'entends bien avec ma sœur.
   I get on well with my sister.

Je ne supporte pas mon beau-père.
   I can't stand my step-dad.

Teenage concerns

●●● Reading

Healthy living

◎ 💲 Here is the label of some medicine you bought in France. Read it and answer the questions to make sure you don't make a serious mistake.

❗ R E M E M B E R
In Reading and Listening, always answer questions in English. Any French in an answer might cost you a mark.

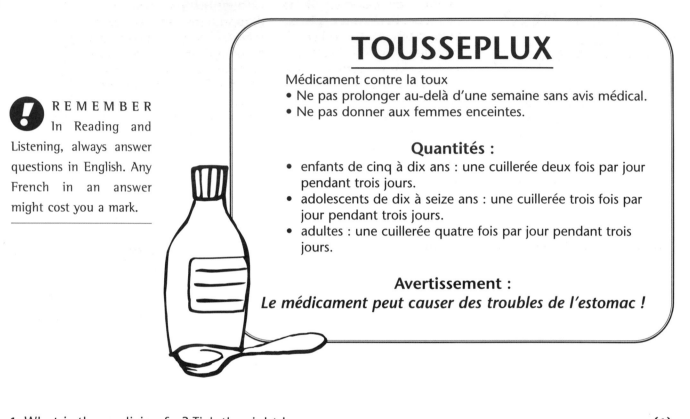

TOUSSEPLUX

Médicament contre la toux
• Ne pas prolonger au-delà d'une semaine sans avis médical.
• Ne pas donner aux femmes enceintes.

Quantités :

• enfants de cinq à dix ans : une cuillerée deux fois par jour pendant trois jours.
• adolescents de dix à seize ans : une cuillerée trois fois par jour pendant trois jours.
• adultes : une cuillerée quatre fois par jour pendant trois jours.

Avertissement :
Le médicament peut causer des troubles de l'estomac !

1 What is the medicine for? Tick the right box.   **(1)**

coughs   ☐

sore heads   ☐

stomach pain   ☐

2 How long can you take the medicine without going to the doctor's?   **(1)**

3 Who should avoid taking the medicine?   **(1)**

4 Since you are a teenager, how many spoonfuls a day should you take?   **(1)**

5 What side effect can the medicine have?   **(1)**

(Total: 5)

The world of work 2

◎ g/c   A teenage magazine reveals the results of a survey on how young people in France imagine the third millennium.

Le troisième millénaire

« Vous êtes plus de trois mille à avoir participé à notre enquête. Bravo, car vous avez une super imagination. Pour 89% d'entre vous, vous voyez l'An 2000 et les années qui vont suivre comme un vrai rêve. Sur Terre, il n'y a plus de chômage, de misère, de guerres, de maladies, ni de pollution. Pour vous déplacer, vous utilisez des rollers à propulsion, des voitures qui volent. Vous voyagez sur plusieurs planètes. Celle que vous préférez est la planète Mars. Dans la vie de tous les jours, un robot s'occupe du ménage, de la cuisine etc. Vous ne travaillez plus. Les robots le font. Les professeurs sont remplacés par des ordinateurs. Vous avez des casques qui vous permettent d'apprendre en quelques minutes. Il y a même des stylos qui écrivent sans faire de faute. La télé a un écran géant et plus de 250 chaînes. Et enfin et surtout, tout le monde va surfer le net sur des écrans portatifs. Bref, c'est le rêve ! »

1 How do 89% of teenagers see the future? Tick the right box. **(1)**

as everything you've ever dreamed of ☐

as a worldwide disaster ☐

no different from today's world ☐

2 Name three things which will no longer exist, according to the article. **(3)**

_____

_____

3 What new kinds of transport are there going to be? **(2)**

_____

_____

4 In everyday life, who will take care of the cleaning and dishes? **(1)**

_____

5 What will replace teachers? **(1)**

_____

6 Name two features that future television sets will have. **(2)**

_____

7 What will everyone be doing? **(1)**

_____

(Total: 11)

REMEMBER In your exam, many of the reading passages are taken from real newspapers and magazines.

REMEMBER Go through the passage (or part of a long passage like this) spotting words you know and words you can guess from English.

REMEMBER In a dictionary it might be difficult to find verbs – don't panic! There are plenty of other words that you will be able to find.

Teenage concerns

AIDS

◎ g/c You read this extract from an article explaining why people with AIDS are people like any others.

REMEMBER Underline in pencil words you think you might have to look up to help you answer the questions.

Le SIDA, ça n'arrive pas qu'aux homosexuels et aux drogués … Tout le monde doit se sentir concerné, car on n'a pas encore trouvé le remède miracle. Mais il ne faut pas non plus paniquer. Le SIDA ne s'attrape pas en serrant la main de quelqu'un ou même en s'embrassant. Il faut qu'il y ait un rapport sexuel non-protégé ou une transfusion de sang affecté. Pour éviter un don de sang contaminé, l'hôpital fait des tests à l'avance, mais il y a une dizaine d'années, des centaines de personnes ont été contaminées à cause de négligences. De toute façon, il faut respecter les personnes atteintes de la maladie et ne pas feindre de les ignorer.
Notre conseil : Abstenez-vous ou protégez-vous !

1 According to the text, why should everyone feel concerned? (1)

2 One can't get AIDS just by kissing. What is the other non-risk action one can do, according to the text? (1)

3 What happened about 10 years ago? Why? (2)

4 What advice are the teenagers given at the end of the text? (2)

(Total: 6)

Negatives

Ne ... pas

To say you do not do something you use **ne ... pas.**

Je ne joue pas de la guitare.   I don't play the guitar.

Note: **ne** changes to **n'** in front of a vowel.

Je n'aime pas les frites.   I don't like chips.

Ne ... plus

Ne ... plus means 'no more' or 'no longer'.
Je ne vais plus à l'école.   I no longer go to school.
Il n'y a plus de devoirs à faire.   There is no more homework to do.

Ne ... rien

Ne ... rien means 'nothing'.
Je n'ai rien gagné au loto.   I didn't win anything in the lottery.
Il n'y a rien à faire à Thurso.   There is nothing to do in Thurso.

Ne ... jamais

Ne ... jamais means 'never'.
Je n'ai jamais regardé ce programme.
I have never watched that programme.

Ne ... ni ... ni

Ne ... ni ... ni means 'neither ... nor'.
Je n'aime ni les gâteaux ni les chocolats.
I don't like cakes or chocolates.

Asking questions

There are several ways to form questions in French.

<u>Forming questions requiring a **oui/non** answer:</u>

• using intonation, with the voice rising at the end of the sentence
Tu vas bien?   Are you OK?
Tu as un animal à la maison?
Have you got a pet?

• using **est-ce que** ...
Est-ce que tu as un animal à la maison?
Have you got a pet?

• changing the word order, with the verb coming first
As-tu un animal à la maison?
Have you got a pet?

Note: changing the word order is more formal than using intonation. It is more often used in writing.

Using question words:

Quand?   When?

Pourquoi?   Why?

Quel?   What?/Which?

Qui?   Who?

Où?   Where?

Lequel?   Which (one)?

Combien?   How much? How many?

Comment?   How?

Quoi?   What?

Qu'est-ce que?   What?

Here are some examples.

Quand arrive-t-il?   When does he arrive?

Où habites-tu?   Where do you live?

Comment vont tes parents?
How are your parents?

65

Teenage concerns

A postcard

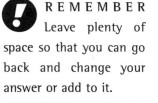 Translate the following postcard into French. The full translation is in the answer section of the book. You don't have to translate in the exam, but this is good practice for Writing.

Dear Annie,
Thank you for your postcard. I'm going to sit my exams next month. I study French, English, maths and science. After the exams, I am going to spend my holiday in France with my parents. I hope it's going to be sunny. In October I'm going to start uni in Edinburgh. Write soon.
Love
Leanne

REMEMBER Leave plenty of space so that you can go back and change your answer or add to it.

Credit writing

Your part-time job and/or pocket money

Look at the *VocabularyZONE* on page 69. Use the sentences and expressions given there to write an essay. Your essay in the final exam should be approximately 200 words. However, quality is far more important than quantity. Why not write about 100 words to start with and get it checked or marked? Your teacher will tell you where you're going wrong.

REMEMBER Write what you have practised many times in class.

A short paragraph

◎ g/c   Write a few sentences about your plans for the future once you have left school. Choose a phrase from each box.

1

après l'école,   after school

quand je quitterai l'école,   when I leave school

plus tard,   later

si j'ai de bonnes notes,   if I have good marks

l'année prochaine,   next year

après les examens,   after the exams

3

avoir un bon travail   have a good job

être bien payé   be well paid

aller à la fac   go to uni

étudier les maths   study maths

travailler à l'étranger   work abroad

voyager   travel

me marier   get married

avoir des enfants   have children

2

je vais   I'm going to

je veux   I want to

j'ai l'intention de (d')   I intend to

je voudrais   I would like to

je ne veux pas   I don't want to

Teenage concerns

Speaking

Speaking about work

You may be asked questions about the job you do after school or at the weekend. Some sample questions are given below. Sample answers are in the answer section of the book. Here are some ideas of what you could say.

Je travaille/ne travaille pas après le collège.   I work/don't work after school.
Il faut que je travaille, parce que je ne reçois pas d'argent de poche.
I have to work as I don't get any pocket money.
Je travaille comme serveur/serveuse.   I work as a waiter/waitress.
Je travaille dans un magasin.   I work in a shop.
Je travaille le week-end seulement.   I only work weekends.
Je reçois trois livres de l'heure.   I get £3 an hour.
C'est bien payé./C'est pas bien payé.   It's good money./The money is awful.
Je commence à quatre heures.   I start at 4.
Je travaille jusqu'à sept heures.   I work until 7.
Je sers les clients.   I serve the customers.
Le travail me plaît/ne me plaît pas.   I like/don't like my work.
Je fais des économies.   I save my money.
J'achète des CD et des fringues.   I buy CDs and clothes (slang for clothes).

> **REMEMBER** Not all the vocabulary is included here – you also have to refer to your notes from school. Have all your notes handy and prepare well in advance.

> **REMEMBER** Try to use as many sentences as possible and give as much information as you can.

Questions you might be asked about work

    Answer these questions using the vocabulary above. Try using some of the joining words given on page 45 as well.

1 *Tu as un petit boulot?*   Do you have a part-time job?

2 *Qu'est-ce que tu fais?*   What do you do?

3 *Où est-ce que tu travailles?*   Where do you work?

4 *Pourquoi est-ce que tu travailles?*   Why do you work?

5 *C'est bien payé?*   Is it well paid?

6 *Tu travailles après l'école?*   Do you work after school?

7 *Est-ce que tu reçois de l'argent de poche?*   Do you get pocket money?

8 *Tu commences à quelle heure?*   What time do you start?

9 *Tu finis à quelle heure?*   When do you finish?

10 *Qu'est-ce que tu fais avec l'argent que tu reçois?*   What do you do with your pay?

> **REMEMBER** It's good to ask a few questions yourself. (See the **GrammarZONE** on how to ask questions on page 65.)

Future work

Here are a few phrases about what kind of work you would like to do in the future.

Que veux tu faire plus tard?
    What do you want to do in the future?

Je veux aller à la fac.   I want to go to uni.

J'ai envie d'étudier les langues.
    I fancy studying languages.

Je voudrais travailler à l'étranger.
    I'd like to work abroad.

J'aimerais travailler en contact avec les gens.
    I'd like to work with people.

Je ne sais pas exactement ce que je voudrais faire.
    I'm not exactly sure what I'd like to do.

Je veux rester à la maison. Je ne veux pas aller à l'université.   I want to stay at home.
    I don't want to go to university.

J'ai l'intention de travailler dans un hôpital.
    I plan to work in a hospital.

Mes parents ont un restaurant. Je peux travailler comme serveur/serveuse si je veux.
    My parents own a restaurant. I can work as a waiter/waitress if I want.

Note that all the underlined phrases can be followed by any verbs in the same form as the one you would find in a dictionary (the infinitive). Look at pages 43 and 51 for more information about this

The world of work

un ingénieur   an engineer

un coiffeur/une coiffeuse   barber/hairdresser

un sapeur-pompier   fireman

un camionneur   lorry driver

une femme/un homme au foyer
    housewife/husband

un formateur/une formatrice   trainer

un conseiller financier/une conseillère financière   financial adviser

un employé/une employée de bureau
    office worker

une puéricultrice   nursery nurse

une sage-femme   midwife

Il/Elle est au chômage.
    He/She is unemployed.

Listening

Future jobs

◎ g/c tv   Watch the video clip where several people are talking about jobs. What jobs would these people like?

Mathieu _____

Marie-Hélène _____

Véronique _____

Julie _____

Caroline _____

Anne _____

Frédéric _____

Geneviève _____

Dominique _____

Régis _____

Virginie _____

Vincent _____

Charlotte _____

(Total: 13)

Sport is important

◎ f/g tv   Watch the clip about sports and write the sports mentioned.

1 _____ (4)

2 _____ (2)

3 _____ (3)

4 _____ (1)

5 _____ (1)

6 _____ (2)

(Total: 13)

Protect the environment

◎ g/c 📺 Watch the video clip where some teenagers are discussing what they do to protect their environment. Tick the correct box.

1 Mame
  a recycles glass ☐
  b avoids dropping litter in the street ☐
  c uses rechargeable batteries ☐

2 Fatima
  a puts litter in a bin ☐
  b walks to school ☐
  c doesn't use CFCs ☐

3 Roxanne
  a uses rechargeable batteries ☐
  b never smokes ☐
  c doesn't waste things that could be re-used ☐

4 Olivier
  a puts litter in a bin ☐
  b doesn't smoke ☐
  c uses rechargeable batteries ☐

5 David
  a re-uses pieces of paper ☐
  b doesn't smoke at all ☐
  c walks to school ☐

6 Anne
  a doesn't smoke ☐
  b uses rechargeable batteries ☐
  c recycles everything at home ☐

7 Caroline
  a sorts her rubbish to be recycled ☐
  b walks to school every day ☐
  c doesn't smoke ☐

(Total: 7)

Teenage concerns

These are listening exercises with a difference. You may not have access to the video, so there are transcripts of listening texts on page 88. Ask a friend or a teacher to record the transcripts on a cassette, then do the activities below.

Dominique's day

◎ *f/g*   Answer these questions about Dominique's daily routine.

1 When does Dominique finally get up?   (1)

2 What does Dominique have for breakfast?   (1)

3 Why does Dominique walk to school?   (1)

4 How far away is the school?   (1)

5 What is the first lesson on a Monday morning?   (1)

6 Why does Dominique not eatg in the school canteen?   (2)

7 Mention three things Dominique does after school.   (3)

(Total: 10)

Patrice on holiday

◎ *f/g*   Ask someone to read the transcript onto cassette. This French boy, Patrice, never goes on holiday. Listen to what he does during the holidays and answer the following questions.

1 Why does he not go on holiday?   (1)

2 How much holiday pocket money does he get?   (1)

3 What two things does he do with the money?   (2)

4 How does he pass the time?   (3)

5 Where does he go if the weather is good?   (1)

6 Where does he go on a Tuesday evening with his parents?   (1)

7 How long do the summer holidays last?   (1)

Christine's holiday

◎ *flg*   Ask someone to read the transcript onto cassette. Listen to the cassette and answer the following questions.

1 Where is Christine going on holiday?   (1)

2 Who is she going with?   (3)

3 When are they leaving?   (1)

4 How will they travel?   (2)

5 How long will they spend there?   (1)

6 What is the weather normally like?   (1)

7 Where are they going to stay?   (1)

8 What can you do in the evenings?   (3)

9 Their daily routine is so different from home. When do they get up?   (1)

10 When do they go to bed?   (1)

(Total: 15)

Sandrine's Scottish holiday

◎ *flg*   Ask someone to read the transcript onto cassette. Listen to the cassette and answer the following questions.

1 Why did Sandrine go to St Monans?   (1)

2 How long did she stay?   (1)

3 How does she describe St Monans?   (1)

4 What was the weather like?   (2)

5 What food did she like best?   (1)

6 Mention three things she did during her stay in Fife.   (3)

7 When does she plan to go back?   (1)

(Total: 10)

Fashion

◉ ⒼⒸ Ask someone to read the transcript onto cassette. Listen to the cassette. Say what each of the eight people think of fashion or brand-named clothes and why.

74

❗ R E M E M B E R
At all levels you are listening for the main point or points, not every single word.

1 (2)

_____

2 (2)

_____

3 (1)

_____

4 (4)

_____

5 (2)

_____

6 (2)

_____

7 (2)

_____

8 (3)

_____

(Total: 18)

The environment

⊙ g/c   Ask someone to read the transcript onto cassette. These teenagers give their opinion on environmental issues. Answer the questions.

1 What should be reduced?   (1)
_____

2 What is the only thing that this person eats?   (1)
_____

3 What must we avoid using?   (1)
_____

4 What should be compulsory for new cars?   (1)
_____

5 What does this person suggest?   (2)
_____

6 What does this person hope for the future?   (1)
_____

7 What should be closed? Why?   (2)
_____

8 What is the energy of the future? Why?   (2)
_____

9 What should we use solar power for?   (1)
_____

(Total: 12)

75

> **❗ REMEMBER**
> In the exam you will hear each item twice. When you are practising you can listen as often as you like.

Work

⊙ f/g   Ask someone to read the transcript onto cassette. Say what each of the people does for a living and where they work.

	job?	where?
1	_____	_____
2	_____	_____
3	_____	_____
4	_____	_____
5	_____	_____
6	_____	_____
7	_____	_____
8	_____	_____
9	_____	_____
10	_____	_____

(Total: 20)

> **❗ REMEMBER**
> Try not to leave blanks. Your guess could be a lucky one and earn you an extra mark.

Extra grammar

Nouns and articles (see page 17)

(?) Look at these words you would find in a dictionary. The (m) tells you it is masculine and the (f) tells you it is feminine. Remember – all nouns in French are either masculine or feminine – even objects!

abricot (m) apricot	*banane (f)* banana, bum bag
bouteille (f) bottle	*cafetière (f)* coffee pot, coffee maker
carotte (f) carrot	*cave (f)* cellar
CD (m) CD	*chambre (f)* bedroom
crêpe (f) pancake	*hôtel (m)* hotel
lit (m) bed	*magazine (m)* magazine
magnétoscope (m) video recorder	*mairie (f)* town hall
oignon (m) onion	*Orangina (m)* Orangina
salle de classe (f) classroom	*sœur (f)* sister
taille-crayon (m) pencil sharpener	*tasse (f)* cup

(◎) Using the dictionary list above, translate the following into French. (The first one is done for you.)

1 a coffee pot *une cafetière*

2 the hotel *un hôtel*

3 the magazines *un magazina*

4 a bum bag *une banane*

5 the apricot *une abricot*

6 the cups *une tasse*

7 a bottle *une bouteille*

8 some carrots_____

9 the onions_____

10 a video recorder_____

(◎) Use the same dictionary list. Put the correct word for 'my' before each French word. Then write the meaning in English beside it. (The first one is done for you.)

1 *ma* chambre my bedroom

2 _____ *banane* _____

3 _____ *magazines* _____

4 _____ *CD* _____

5 _____ *magnétoscope* _____

6 _____ *sœurs* _____

7 _____ *crêpe* _____

8 _____ *Orangina* _____

Adjectives (see page 21)

◎ Put in the correct adjective. Choose from the box below. Use each adjective only once.

1 J'habite un _____ village à la campagne. Il y a 35 habitants.

2 Nous avons une Ford, mais je préfère les voitures _____.

3 J'ai un _____ frère de trente ans, et moi, j'ai quinze ans.

4 Il y a beaucoup de choses à voir dans ma ville. Elle est très _____.

5 Mon frère va à l'université de Lyon. Il est très _____.

6 Les meilleures pizzas sont les pizzas _____.

| allemandes | belle | grand | intelligent | italiennes | petit |

Prepositions (see page 37)

◎ Put in the correct word for 'to' and 'in'.

1 ____ Edimbourg   2 ____ Pays-Bas (plural)

3 ____ Etats-Unis (plural)   4 ____ France

5 ____ Espagne   6 ____ Paris

7 ____ Portugal (masculine)   8 ____ Pays de Galles (masculine)

Making comparisons (see page 39)

◎ When comparing things or people, use **plus** + the adjective. Complete these comparisons using the correct adjective from the box below.

1 *Mon frère est _____ _____ que mon père.*

2 *Mes cousins sont _____ _____ que moi.*

3 *Notre voiture était _____ _____ que la voiture de ma tante.*

4 *La Tour Eiffel est _____ _____ que l'Arc de Triomphe.*

5 *Mes sœurs sont _____ _____ que mes frères.*

| âgés | chère | grandes | haute | intelligent |

Subject pronouns (see page 43)

◎ Put in the correct pronoun. Choose from the box beside.

1 _____ *vais à l'école à pied.*   2 *En été, _____ fait toujours beau.*

3 *Où travaillent-_____, tes parents?* 4 _____ *aimez l'Ecosse, madame?*

5 *Ma sœur? _____ écoute ses CD.*

je (I)	nous (we)
tu (you)	vous (you)
il (he, it)	ils (they)
elle (she, it)	elles (they)
on (we)	

Verbs – infinitive (see page 43)

◎ In each of the sentences below, the verb is followed by a second verb in the infinitive. Sometimes there is an extra **à** or **de** before the infinitive.

Complete the sentences by choosing from the box. The English translation of each sentence is given to help you.

aller
de faire
à parler
à pleuvoir
rester
de sortir

1 *J'adore _____ en ville.*
   I love going into town.

2 *Ma mère apprend _____ espagnol.*
   My mother is learning to speak Spanish.

3 *En Ecosse, il faut _____ à l'école jusqu'à 3h30.*
   In Scotland you have to stay at school until 3.30.

4 *Hier, j'ai oublié _____ mes devoirs.*
   Yesterday I forgot to do my homework.

5 *Vous avez décidé _____ ce soir?*
   Have you decided to go out tonight?

6 *Ah non! Il commence _____.*
   Oh no! It's starting to rain.

Verbs – present tense (see page 47)

◎ Put in the correct part of the verb in the **present tense**. (Look back at page 45 if you need a reminder.)

1 Tous les jours, je _____ au collège à pied. (aller)

2 Le soir, mes parents _____ la télé. (regarder)

3 Quand j'ai le temps, j'_____ mes CD. (écouter)

4 Je suis désolé. Je ne _____ pas aller à la boum. (pouvoir)

5 Tu _____ sortir ce soir? (vouloir)

6 Vous _____ les escargots? (aimer)

7 Je _____ aller à l'hôpital (devoir)

8 On _____ du sport le lundi. (faire)

9 Je ___ _____ à dix heures. (se coucher)

10 Nous _____ _____ tard le week-end. (se lever)

Reflexive verbs – present tense (see page 47)

◎ Use these verbs in six sentences to talk about yourself.

se lever (to get up)   s'amuser (to have fun)

s'habiller (to get dressed)   se doucher (to have a shower)

se coucher (to go to bed)   se promener (to go for a walk)

Example: *Je me lève à huit heures.*

Modal verbs – present tense (see page 51)

◎ Translate the following sentences into French using part of the verb aller to show that they are in the future. Parts of the sentences have been done for you.

1 *Samedi, je _____ aller en ville.* (must)

2 *Maman, est-ce que je _____ regarder une vidéo?* (can)

3 *Tu _____ sortir ce soir?* (want to)

4 *Mon grand-père _____ parler allemand.* (knows how to)

5 *A Stirling, on _____ visiter le château.* (can)

6 *Nous _____ attendre la fin du match.* (have to)

7 *Je ne _____ pas faire de l'équitation.* (want to)

8 *Je ne _____ pas nager.* (know how to)

| devons | dois | peut | peux | sais | sait | veux | veux |

Verbs – future tense (see page 51)

◎   Translate the following sentences into French using part of the verb **aller** to show that they are in the future. Parts of the sentences have been done for you.

1 Tomorrow I'm going to go into town.

   Demain, ____ _____ aller en ville.

2 Next week my mother is going to start her new job.

   La semaine prochaine, ____ _____ _____ commencer son nouveau travail.

3 In the future I'm going to work abroad.

   Plus tard, ____ _____ travailler à l'étranger.

4 If I have time I'll visit Strasbourg.

   Si j'ai le temps, ____ _____ visiter Strasbourg.

5 Are you going to go to uni?

   Est-ce que _____ _____ aller à la fac?

6 We're going to play football after school.

   _____ _____ jouer au football après l'école.

Verbs – perfect tense (see page 57)

◎   Complete the sentences in the past tense.

1 J'____ _____ mon travail. (finir)

2 Nous _____ _____ d'aller en France. (décider)

3 Qu'est-ce que tu ____ _____ aujourd'hui? (manger)

4 Mes copains et mes copines _____ _____ la maison à huit heures. (quitter)

5 Ma mère ____ _____ en ville. (aller)

6 Hier, j'____ _____ du sport au collège. (faire)

7 Dimanche, ils ____ _____ _____ à onze heures. (se lever)

80

Negatives (see page 67)

◎ Make the following sentences negative. Don't forget to shorten **ne** to **n'** before a verb which begins with a vowel.

1 Je vais en ville avec mes copains.

2 Ma tante parle français.

3 Le samedi soir, mes parents mangent à la maison.

4 Tu aimes les escargots?

5 Mon petit frère joue au hockey.

6 Mes grands-parents habitent en Ecosse.

Asking questions (see page 67)

◎ There are several ways of asking questions in French. Choose two different ways to make each of these sentences into a question.

1 On joue de la cornemuse en Ecosse.

2 Tes parents travaillent.

3 Les Ecossais portent le kilt.

4 On peut visiter la cathédrale.

5 Tu aimes la musique rap.

Answers to extra grammar

Nouns and articles: Translate ... (page 76)

1 une cafetière, 2 l'hôtel, 3 les magazines, 4 une banane,
5 l'abricot, 6 les tasses, 7 une bouteille, 8 des carottes,
9 les oignons, 10 un magnétoscope.

Nouns and articles: Put the correct word for my ... (page 76)

1 ma, my bedroom, 2 ma, my banana, 3 mes, my
magazines, 4 mon/mes, my CD/CDs, 5 mon, my video
recorder, 6 mes, my sisters, 7 ma, my pancake, 8 mon, my
Orangina.

Adjectives (page 77)

1 petit, 2 allemandes, 3 grand, 4 belle, 5 intelligent,
6 italiennes

Prepositions (page 77)

1 à, 2 aux, 3 aux, 4 en, 5 en, 6 à, 7 au, 8 au

Making comparisons (page 77)

1 Mon frère est plus intelligent que mon père.

2 Mes cousins sont plus âgés que moi.

3 Notre voiture était plus chère que la voiture de ma
tante.

4 La Tour Eiffel est plus haute que l'Arc de Triomphe.

5 Mes sœurs sont plus grandes que mes frères.

Subject pronouns (page 77)

1 Je, 2 il, 3 ils, 4 Vous, 5 Elle

Verbs – infinitive (page 78)

1 aller, 2 à parler, 3 rester, 4 de faire, 5 de sortir,
6 à pleuvoir

Verbs – present tense (page 78)

1 vais, 2 regardent, 3 écoute, 4 peux, 5 veux, 6 aimez,
7 dois, 8 fait, 9 me couche, 10 nous levons

Reflexive verbs – present tense (page 79)

Sample answers

Je me lève à sept heures.

Le samedi, je m'amuse à la piscine.

Le week-end, je m'habille en jean et pull-over.

Je me douche chaque matin.

D'habitude, je me couches à dix heures.

En été, je me promène avec mes copains.

Modal verbs – present tense (page 79)

1 dois, 2 peux, 3 veux, 4 sait, 5 peut, 6 devons, 7 veux,
8 sais

Verbs – future tense (page 80)

1 je vais, 2 ma mère va, 3 je vais, 4 je vais, 5 tu vas/vous
allez, 6 nous allons/on va

Verbs – perfect tense (page 80)

1 ai fini, 2 avons décidé, 3 as mangé, 4 ont quitté, 5 est
allée, 6 ai fait, 7 se sont levés

Negatives (page 81)

1 Je ne vais pas en ville avec mes copains.

2 Ma tante ne parle pas français.

3 Le samedi soir, mes parents ne mangent pas à la maison.

4 Tu n'aimes pas les escargots?

5 Mon petit frère ne joue pas au hockey.

6 Mes grands-parents n'habitent pas en Ecosse.

Asking questions (page 81)

1 On joue de la cornemuse en Ecosse?

   Est-ce qu'on joue de la cornemuse en Ecosse?

   Joue-t-on de la cornemuse en Ecosse?

2 Tes parents travaillent?

   Est-ce que tes parents travaillent?

   Tes parents, travaillent-ils?

3 Les Ecossais portent le kilt?

   Est-ce que les Ecossais portent le kilt?

   Les Ecossais, portent-ils le kilt?

4 On peut visiter la cathédrale?

   Est-ce qu'on peut visiter la cathédrale?

   Peut-on visiter la cathédrale?

5 Tu aimes la musique rap?

   Est-ce que tu aimes la musique rap?

   Aimes-tu la musique rap?

Answers

General questions (page 3)

Sample answers

1 *Généralement, je reste à la maison parce que j'ai beaucoup de devoirs. Le samedi soir, je sors avec mes copains/copines*
Normally I stay at home because I've got lots of homework. On Saturday nights I go out with my friends.

2 *Quand je vais au collège, je me lève tous les matins à sept heures. En vacances, j'adore faire la grasse matinée. Je me lève vers onze heures.*
In term time I get up at seven every morning. On holiday I love having a lie in. I get up at about eleven o'clock.

3 *Le jour de mon anniversaire, j'invite des copains et des copines. On regarde une vidéo et on écoute des CD.*
On my birthday I invite friends round. We watch a video and listen to CDs.

4 *Je déteste mon collège. Il n'est pas moderne et il n'y a pas de piscine.*
I hate my school. It's not modern and there's no swimming pool.

5 *C'est une ville touristique. Il y a plein de châteaux et de musées.*
It's a tourist town. There are plenty of castles and museums.

6 *Il n'y a rien à faire pour les jeunes. / Tous les samedis, il y a un film à la MJC. Il y a beaucoup de choses à faire au collège le soir. On peut apprendre la cuisine.*
There's nothing for young people to do. / Every Saturday there's a film at the Youth Centre. There's lots to do at school in the evenings. You can learn how to cook.

7 *En Ecosse, on mange trop de matière grasse (par exemple des frites, des chips). En France, on mange beaucoup de pain et on boit du vin. En Ecosse, c'est le whisky.*
In Scotland we eat too much fat (e.g. chips, crisps). In France they eat lots of bread and drink wine. In Scotland it's whisky.

8 *Je ne reçois pas d'argent de poche parce que je travaille tous les jours après le collège de quatre heures à cinq heures et demie.*
I don't get any pocket money because I work every day after school from four until five thirty.

9 *Ça dépend. Si j'ai beaucoup de devoirs, je rentre à la maison. Sinon, je vais en ville. J'adore faire du lèche-vitrine.*
It all depends. If I've got a lot of homework I go home. Otherwise I go into town. I love window-shopping.

10 *Ma mère travaille à la Poste. Mon père est homme au foyer.*
My mother works at the post office. My father is a house husband.

11 *Je travaille comme serveur/serveuse dans un restaurant. Ce n'est pas bien payé, mais c'est mieux que rien.*
I work as a waiter/waitress in a restaurant. It's not well paid but it's better than nothing.

12 *Je préfère partir en vacances avec mes parents. Toute la famille est très sportive. On fait beaucoup de sports.*
I prefer going away with my parents. The whole family is very sporty. We do a lot of sport.

13 *En ce moment, je ne sais pas exactement. Si j'ai de bonnes notes, je voudrais aller à l'université. J'ai l'intention d'étudier les sciences.*
At the moment I don't know exactly. If I get good grades I'd like to go to university. I intend studying science.

14 *Une fois par semaine, je mange au self, mais je ne l'aime pas. Je préfère aller en ville où je m'achète quelque chose à manger.*
Once a week I eat in the school canteen but I don't like it. I prefer to go into town and buy myself something to eat.

15 *J'habite assez loin de l'école. Alors, je prends le bus, sauf quand il fait beau. Puis je viens au collège en vélo. C'est pratique.*
I live quite far away from school. So I catch the bus, except when the weather's good. Then I come to school on my bike. It's handy.

Daily life

Reading

Reading a postcard from a friend (page 10)

The six mistakes are: 14 (he is 15), 11th August (it's on the 12th), very small (he's quite small), grey eyes (he's got green eyes), my brother (it's his sister), at another school (at his own school).

Moving house (page 12)

1 A and C, 2 electric heating, 3 because someone died, 4 because the price can be negociated, 5 because the property is situated not far from them, 6 C

Weekly chores (page 13)

Monday – 6, Tuesday – 2, Wednesday – 7, Thursday – 5, Friday – 3, Saturday – 1, Sunday – 4

Trouve l'intrus (page 13)

1 *chambre* – it is a room, the rest are accommodation

2 *tante* – it is a female, the rest are all males

3 *professeur* – it is a teacher while the rest are subjects

4 *magnétoscope* – it is a video recorder/player,
   the rest are to do with computer and video games

Pocket money (page 14)

1 every week, 2 fifty francs, 3 goes to cinema or football match, 4 CDs or video games, 5 it's badly paid

Wordsearch (page 14)

video recorder – *magnétoscope*, week – *semaine*, music – *musique*, savings – *économies*, swimming pool – *piscine*, month – *mois*, to sell – *vendre*, to rent – *louer*, furnished – *meublé*, to buy – *acheter*

M	A	G	N	E	T	O	S	C	O	P	E
U	A	J	K	C	W	K	E	B	M	I	X
S	L	A	F	O	X	Q	M	K	E	S	C
I	O	C	H	N	Y	H	A	E	U	C	L
Q	U	H	M	O	I	S	I	J	B	I	U
U	E	E	G	M	G	I	N	A	L	N	Y
E	R	T	H	I	Z	T	E	V	E	E	O
W	Z	E	V	E	N	D	R	E	V	D	D
U	I	R	C	S	K	O	P	A	Z	Q	

Daily routine 1 (page 16)

1B, 2J, 3H, 4K, 5C, 6A, 7G, 8L, 9E, 10I, 11F, 12D

Daily routine 2 (page 18)

1 at about 7.15, 2 cereal, 3 run because he misses his bus, 4 because in some other French schools they start even earlier at 8am, 5 McDonald's, because the food at the canteen is not brilliant, 6 slices of bread and jam and hot chocolate, 7 doing homework, 8 they have it at a later time than in Scotland, between 7pm and 8pm, 9 the news, 10 stay out or watch TV later

Timetable (page 19)

1 three times, 2 at the school canteen, 3a Mondays to Thursdays, 3b from 10am to 3.30pm, 4 (see the timetable below)

Mon	Tue	Wed	Thu	Fri	Sat
French	free	PE	hist/geog	English	PSE
German	art	music	English	maths	biology
maths	English	technol.	French	free	hist/geog
physics	biology	free	French	technol.	-

PE	French	physics	ICT	art	
PE	hist/geog	free	German	free	
-	English	French	-	German	
-	PSE	-	-	maths	

French schools (page 20)

1 six; 2 they go at the age of eleven; there is a different teacher for each subject; 3 in terminale (final year), at about 18; 4 go on to university or find a job; 5 repeat the year; 6 sixteen

Birthday presents (page 22)

Two video games; four of us can play together; Brazil; they are the best; find treasure on an island; kill the pirates; young people worldwide; homework; information; surf the net; send each other e-mails

Films (page 23)

The film is called Titanic.

1A, 2C, 3C, 4B – it is drug-related, 5 unberable suspense

Writing

Postcard (page 24)

See page 10 for a sample answer.

Writing practice (page 24)

Sample answers

Name	Je m'appelle Marie-Claire.
Age	J'ai quinze ans.
Brothers and sisters	J'ai deux sœurs et un frère.
Hobbies	Je fais de la natation et je joue au basket.
Your daily routine	Je me lève à huit heures et je me couche à onze heures.
School	Ma matière préférée au collège est l'EPS.
Pets	Je n'ai pas d'animal à la maison.
Things you don't like doing	Je déteste sortir la poubelle.
Weekend	Le week-end, je sors avec mes copains.
Holidays	Pendant les grandes vacances, je vais chez mes grands-parents.

Letter (page 25)

Words to fill in the blanks: *ans, premier, grande, blonds, frère, vingt, biologie, divorcés, kilomètres, ingénieur, numéro, chambre, chez, maison, enfants, adore.*

Listening

Clémentine's family (page 28)

Her mother's name:	Chantal
Her mother's age:	43
Her mother's job:	librarian
Her mother's hobby:	crosswords
Her brother's name:	Emile
Her brother's age:	11
Number of pets:	40 rats
	20 mice
Her father leaves at:	6.30am
Her father works at:	the post-office
Her father's hobby after work:	French bowls

Describing a town (page 29)

1	agréable	pleasant/nice
2	beau (masc.), belle (fem.)	beautiful/lovely
3	culturel(le)	full of culture
4	petit(e)	small
5	tranquille	quiet
6	touristique	touristy
7	sympathique	nice
8	varié(e)	varied
9	gai(e)	pleasant:
10	vivant(e)	lively
11	joli(e)	pretty/nice
12	calme	quiet
13	charmant(e)	full of charm
14	moderne	modern
15	dynamique	dynamic/lively.

Pocket money (page 29)

1 no pocket money or works, 2 gets pocket money or babysits, 3 delivers papers on a Saturday, 4 gets pocket money or works in a shop, 5 gets pocket money or doesn't find it is enough, 6 gets 150F a month from parents or she uses it for leisure activities, 7 gets 600F a month or has to pay for everything, 8 doesn't get pocket money or does babysitting/can go out

Favourite subjects (page 30)

1 biology, 2 biology, 3 biology, 4 physics, 5 PE/sport, 6 maths, 7 music, 8 French, 9 English

Arranging to go out (page 30)

1 a film, 2 seen it, 3 any three: football, swimming, cycling, sport, 4 Monday, Tuesday, Wednesday

Listening to the radio (page 31)

1b, 2a, 3a, 4b, 5a or b, 6c, 7a

Holidays and travel

Reading

Reading about directions (page 32)

1 first left, 2 park, 3 smoke, 4: animals not allowed, 5 feed the animals, 6 free reserved car park for restaurant patrons only, 7 get a fine, 8 at the end of the corridor

Weather forecast (page 34)

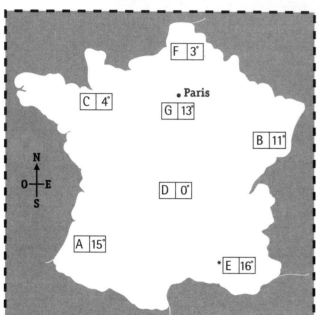

* G also possible

Travel (page 35)

1 a week, 2a 5650F, 2b 5580F, 2c 5200F, 3 6 nights, 4 a helicopter flight and a visit to Alcatraz, 5 daily

Metro (page 35)

1 doors must be shut, 2 any two: open doors before the train stops, prevent the doors from shutting, lean out of the windows, 3 automatically, 4 get a fine

Letter from a hotel (page 36)

1 Sevran, 2 15th July, 3 from 17th August to 24th August, 4 2nd floor, 5 a canal, 6 600F a night, 7 yes, 8 20 minutes by car

Eating out 1 (page 38)

1 every day except Tuesday, 2 29F, 3 26F, 4 chips, 5 10F

Eating out 2 (page 40)

1 a huge buffet, 2 Greece, Algeria, Spain, France, 3 cakes/pastries, 4 succulent flavours, 5 a starter, a main dish, a dessert to choose from the menu

At the supermarket (page 41)

1A, 2F, 3B, 4C, 5E, 6A, 7C, 8D, 9G, 10H

Trouve l'intrus (page 41)

1 un jus de pomme (apple juice, to drink and not to eat), 2 un bateau (doesn't fly), 3 service compris (not accommodation), 4 un chemisier (not men's clothing), 5 tournez à droite (the others are straight on)

Clothes (page 42)

1 any five: dress, trousers, boots, skirt, blouse, shirt, silk tie, raincoat, jumpers, 2c, 3 79F, 4 16th July, 5 Louvre, 6 late opening until 10pm

Writing

More complicated essay (page 44)

Pendant les vacances, je me lève à dix heures du matin parce que j'adore faire la grasse matinée. En général, je prends un petit déjeuner avec des fruits et je bois un jus d'orange. Après le petit déjeuner, je prends une douche et je m'habille. Quand il fait beau, je quitte l'hôtel pour aller à la plage où je me bronze pendant deux heures. Vers midi, je prends le déjeuner au restaurant, près du centre-ville. L'après-midi, je fais les magasins avec ma sœur qui cherche des souvenirs pour la famille. Je préfère regarder des magazines. On boit un café et on mange un gâteau. Ensuite, on rentre à l'hôtel, où on dîne à huit heures après l'apéro. Je regarde la télé jusqu'à minuit ou je joue au baby-foot. Avant de me coucher, je mange un bol de céréales.

A postcard from your holidays (page 46)

Sample answer

Chère Sophie,

Je suis en vacances à Paris. Je suis arrivé mercredi.

C'est super ici! Il fait chaud. Tous les jours, je visite des musées.

Le matin, je me lève à neuf heures. Le soir, je me couche à minuit.

A bientot.   Alex

A letter from Béatrice (page 49)

ta, Mon, ma, Mes, Mon, sa, leurs, Notre, Mon, mon, Son, tes, Ton, ta, ton

Listening

Hotel Canella Beach (page 52)

Number of bedrooms:	152
Location of hotel:	near the beach
Breakfast menu:	fruit, bread, yoghurt, cheese, ham
Facilities:	pool, restaurant, sea, bowls, children's club, sailing club, boating

Booking a room (page 52)

He wants a room booked for <u>three</u> nights, from <u>Monday 7th</u> to <u>Wednesday 9th</u>.

He wants a room with a <u>bath</u>.

Breakfast costs <u>45 francs</u>.

His name is spelt <u>M I R J O L</u>.

Statistics (page 53)

1 Paris – Le Mans: 123 francs

2 10 carriages

3 116 First Class seats

4 369 Second Class seats

5 40,000 passengers per day

6 15 return trips per day

7 Normal speed: 300km/h

8 Paris – Le Mans: 50 minutes

Travelling by train (page 54)

1b, 2b, 3a, 4a, 5a, 6a

Going on holiday (page 54)

1b, 2a, 3b, 4c, 5b, 6a

Shopping (page 55)

<u>Liste d'achats</u>

2–3 aubergines

<u>500g</u> courgettes

<u>1</u> kg de tomates

3 <u>oignons</u>

de l'ail

Clothes (page 55)

Florent	T-shirts, sweatshirts
Vincent	jeans, T-shirts, pullover
David	jeans
Caroline	short skirts, tights, jacket, scarf, hat
Marie-Hélène	jeans, jumper
Frédéric	casual clothes

Teenage concerns

Reading

La vie de Diana (page 56)

1 in the south, 2 at the age of 16, 3 looked after babies/nanny, 4 it is her first son's birth(day), 5 she divorced Prince Charles, 6 any three: the ill, the poor, children, war victims

Racial prejudice (page 58)

any seven of the following: motorbike – Korea; rice – China; couscous – Algeria; Olympic Games – Greece; coffee – Colombia; knife – Switzerland; shirt – Tahiti; walkman – Taiwan; holidays – Portugal, Spain or Africa; movies – America; take-aways – India

How can anyone be racist?

The world of work 1 (page 59)

1a he worked hard and got good results, 1b he also was a bit of a nuisance, 2 a doctor – to 'mend' people, 3 18 years old, 4 10 years, 5 because of an injury, 6 every night apart from Tuesdays

The environment (page 60)

positive: 3 (unleaded petrol), 5 (CFC free), 7 (ozone friendly), 9 (no colourings or preservatives)

negative: 1 (pollution), 2 (nuclear power), 4 (greenhouse effect), 6 (chemicals), 8 (exhaust fumes), 10 (insecticide)

Wordsearch (page 60)

pile, acide, caméscope, pollution, recyclage, déchets, ozone, ordures, plomb, dopage.

R	A	S	A	R	D	O	P	P	D
O	C	A	M	E	S	C	O	P	E
P	I	L	E	C	O	D	L	U	C
L	D	S	B	Y	R	O	L	Z	H
O	E	A	A	C	D	P	U	R	E
M	G	J	F	L	U	A	T	N	T
B	H	L	I	A	R	G	I	Q	S
E	M	O	K	G	E	E	O	C	Q
O	Z	O	N	E	S	R	N	P	D

Healthy living (page 62)

1 coughs, 2 one week, 3 expectant mothers, 4 three, 5 stomach disorder

The world of work 2 (page 63)

1 as everything you've ever dreamed of, 2 any three: unemployment, poverty, wars, disease, pollution, 3 motorized roller blades/skates, flying cars, 4 a robot, 5 computers, 6 giant screen, more than 250 channels, 7 surfing the net on their laptops

AIDS (page 64)

1 as yet there's no cure and it doesn't only affect homosexuals and drug addicts, 2 shake somebody's hand, 3 some people got contaminated through a blood transfusion; the blood hadn't been checked properly, 4 no sex or use some form of protection

Writing

A postcard (page 66)

Chère Annie,

Merci pour ta carte postale. Je vais avoir mes examens le mois prochain. J'étudie le français, l'anglais, les maths et les sciences. Après les examens, je vais passer les vacances en France avec mes parents. J'espère qu'il va faire du soleil. En octobre, je vais commencer à la fac à Edimbourg.

Ecris-moi vite.

Bises

Leanne

A short paragraph (page 67)

Sample answers

Quand je quitterai l'école, je voudrais travailler à l'étranger.

L'année prochaine, j'ai l'intention de voyager.

Plus tard, je veux me marier.

Speaking

Questions you might be asked about work (page 68)

Sample answers

1   Oui, je travaille le week-end dans un restaurant italien.

Yes, I work weekends in an Italian restaurant.

2 Je fais la vaisselle en cuisine, ou je prends les réservations au téléphone.
   I do the dishes in the kitchen or take bookings on the phone.

3 Le restaurant où je travaille est dans le centre-ville, en face de l'hôtel de ville.
   The restaurant I work in is in the town centre, opposite the town hall.

4 Je travaille parce que j'adore avoir mon propre argent.
   I work because I love having my own money.

5 Je reçois trois livres cinquante de l'heure.
   I get £3.50 an hour.

6 Non, j'ai beaucoup de devoirs, donc je travaille seulement le samedi soir.
   No, I have lots of homework, so I just work Saturday nights.

7 Non, je ne reçois pas d'argent de poche, mais mes parents m'achètent mes vêtements.
   No, I don't get pocket money, but my parents buy my clothes.

8 Ça dépend. S'il y a beaucoup de clients, je commence à six heures. Sinon, c'est huit heures.
   That depends. If it's busy, I start at six. If not, it's eight o'clock.

9 Je finis à minuit et demi. Le restaurant ferme à minuit. Je rentre à la maison en taxi.
   I finish at half past twelve. The restaurant shuts at midnight. I get a taxi home.

10 Mes parents m'achètent mes vêtements. Donc, je dépense mon argent en CD ou en cadeaux pour des copains. Après Noël, je fais des économies.
   My parents buy my clothes. So I spend my money on CDs or presents for friends. After Christmas, I put my money in the bank.

Listening

Future jobs (page 70)

Mathieu	film director
Marie-Hélène	teacher
Véronique	teacher (political science)
Julie	journalist
Caroline	stage manager
Anne	doctor
Frédéric	actor
Geneviève	lawyer (solicitor)
Dominique	(industrial) engineer
Régis	actor
Virginie	nurse
Vincent	designer
Charlotte	archaeologist

Sport is important (page 71)

1 swimming, running (jogging), martial arts, athletics
2 skiing, jogging
3 football, skiing, sailing
4 football
5 horse-riding
6 dancing, basketball

Protect the environment (page 71)

1b, 2a, 3c, 4a, 5a, 6c, 7a

Extra listening exercises

Dominique's day (page 72)

Tous les matins, je me réveille vers six heures. Je déteste les matins. Je me lève à six heures et demie.

Le matin, je n'aime pas manger. Je ne mange rien au petit déjeuner.

Il faut aller au collège à pied. Je suis toujours en retard et je rate le bus.

Le collège est assez loin de chez moi. Il est à huit kilomètres de notre village.

Le premier cours le lundi matin, c'est l'histoire/géo.

Je ne mange jamais au self. Je n'aime pas la cuisine et je préfère m'acheter un MacDo.

Le collège finit à cinq heures. Je vais en ville où je fais les magasins.

Je suis un(e) passionné(e) de natation. Donc, je vais à la piscine tous les jours.

Patrice on holiday (page 73)

Je ne pars jamais en vacances. Je préfère rester à la maison.

Je reçois beaucoup d'argent – de mes parents et de mes grands-parents. Deux mille francs.

Avec l'argent que je reçois, je m'achète des CD et je fais des économies.

J'adore sortir avec mes copains. On va en ville, on va au ciné ou à la patinoire.

S'il fait chaud, je vais à la piscine. Près de chez nous, il y a une piscine de plein air.

Tous les mardis soirs, je vais chez mes grands-parents avec mes parents. C'est une sorte de tradition.

J'adore les grandes vacances. Pas de collège pendant deux mois et demi – oui, dix semaines!

Christine's holiday (page 72)

Je m'appelle Christine. Cet été, je vais en Espagne.

Je pars en vacances avec ma mère, mon grand-père et ma sœur.

J'adore l'Espagne. Nous partons le deux juillet.

Nous prenons l'autocar jusqu'à Manchester, et puis on prend l'avion.

On va rester huit jours en Espagne.

En été, il fait très chaud, trente degrés.

Moi, je déteste les hôtels. On va louer un appartement au bord de la mer.

Pendant la journée, on va à la plage. Le soir, on peut aller à la discothèque, aller au restaurant ou rester dans l'appartement.

On se lève à midi, et on se couche vers trois heures du matin.

Sandrine's Scottish holiday (page 73)

Pourquoi St Monans? Ma correspondante écossaise habite à St Monans. Elle s'appelle Emma Reekie.

Moi, j'habite au sud de la France. C'est loin de St Monans. Donc, j'y suis restée cinq semaines.

St Monans est un grand village.

Pendant mon séjour, il a fait froid, mais le ciel était bleu.

Je n'ai pas aimé la cuisine écossaise, mais le poisson, c'était délicieux.

Un jour, je suis allée au théâtre. J'ai visité un château. Il y avait une grande ferme près de St Monans. J'ai fait une sortie en bateau et j'ai fait de la pêche.

Et quand est-ce que je vais retourner à St Monans? Jamais! Jamais de ma vie! Je n'aime pas les villages.

Fashion (page 74)

1 Moi, je m'achète des vêtements de marque. C'est plus cher, mais la qualité est vraiment meilleure.

2 Je ne comprends pas les gens qui achètent des vêtements de grandes marques. C'est trop cher, car on paie le nom.

3 Moi, parfois, j'achète des marques si ça me plaît, mais ça ne me dérange pas de porter des vêtements plus ordinaires.

4 Quel est l'intérêt d'acheter une marque? C'est cher et tout le monde porte les mêmes fringues.
C'est idiot, non?

5 Je ne pourrais pas sortir sans porter des vêtements de marque. C'est vraiment classe.

6 Au lieu d'acheter des vêtements de marque trop chers, je préfère dépenser mon argent au cinéma.

7 J'adore faire les magasins et acheter les vêtements à la mode. C'est sympa.

8 La mode, c'est pas mon truc. Ma mère m'achète tous mes vêtements, alors je n'ai pas le choix, de toute façon.

The environment (page 75)

1 Je crois qu'on devrait réduire les émissions de gaz d'échappement.

2 Je ne mange que des produits sans colorant ni conservateur.

3 On doit éviter d'utiliser les produits contenant du CFC.

4 L'essence sans plomb devrait être obligatoire sur les nouvelles voitures.

5 On devrait recycler le papier et le verre.

6 J'espère qu'un vaccin contre le SIDA sera trouvé d'ici à dans cinq ans.

7 Le nucléaire est, à mon avis, trop dangereux. Il faut fermer les centrales.

8 Le nucléaire, c'est l'avenir de l'énergie et ça ne pollue pas autant que le charbon ou le gaz.

9 Il faudrait utiliser l'énergie solaire pour éclairer les maisons, grâce à des panneaux solaires.

Work (page 75)

1 Je travaille comme caissier dans un hypermarché.

2 Moi, je suis avocate au palais de justice.

3 Mon boulot à moi, c'cst éboucur. Je suis dans la rue à sept heures du matin.

4 Mon père est cheminot. Il conduit les trains.

5 Ma copine voyage en avion tous les jours. Elle est hôtesse de l'air.

6 Elle est décoratrice d'intérieur. Elle va chez les gens.

7 Jacques est gérant d'un restaurant.

8 Sa tante est femme au foyer. Elle est presque toujours à la maison.

9 Zidoue est footballeur professionnel. Il joue sur tous les terrains du monde.

10 Il est chirurgien-dentiste. Il travaille dans un cabinet dentaire.

Answers to extra listening exercises

Dominique's day (page 72)

1 6.30, 2 nothing, 3 misses the bus, 4 eight kilometres, 5 history/geography, 6 doesn't like the food, prefers a McDonald's, 7 goes into town, goes (window-)shopping, goes swimming

Patrice on holiday (page 73)

1 prefers to stay at home, 2 2000 francs, 3 buys CDs, saves, 4 any three: goes out with friends, goes into town, goes to the cinema, goes skating, 5 to the (open-air) pool, 6 to his grandparents, 7 two and a half months (ten weeks)

Christine's holiday (page 72)

1 Spain, 2 mother, grandfather, sister, 3 2nd July, 4 coach (bus) and plane, 5 one week (eight days), 6 (very) hot or 30°, 7 flat (apartment) or at the seaside, 8 go to disco, eat out, stay in the flat, 9 midday, 10 (about) 3am

Sandrine's Scottish holiday (page 73)

1 her penfriend lives there, 2 five weeks, 3 a large village, 4 cold, blue sky, 5 fish, 6 any three: theatre, castle, farm, out in a boat, went fishing, 7 never

Fashion (page 74)

1 buys brand-named clothes; quality is better, 2 can't understand people buying brand names; it's dear because of the name, 3 not bothered either way, 4 can't see the point in buying brand names; it's dear; everyone buys the same things; it's stupid, 5 can't go out without them; they're smart, 6 instead of buying expensive clothes, prefers going to cinema, 7 loves shopping for fashionable clothes; it's great, 8 fashion isn't his/her thing; mother buys clothes; no choice anyway

The environment (page 75)

1 exhaust gases, 2 food without colouring or preservatives, 3 products containing CFCs, 4 unleaded petrol, 5 recycling paper and glass, 6 that there will be a cure (vaccine) for AIDS, 7 nuclear power stations, too dangerous, 8 nuclear power, doesn't pollute as much as coal or gas, 9 lighting houses

Work (page 75)

1 checkout operator, hypermarket, 2 lawyer, court, 3 dustman, street, 4 train driver, train, 5 air hostess, plane, 6 interior designer, people's houses, 7 manager, restaurant, 8 housewife, home, 9 professional footballer, pitches all over the world, 10 dental surgeon, dentist's surgery